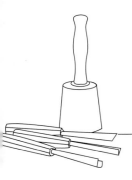

# RELIEF CARVING

By W.F. Judt

FOX BOOKS
Fox Chapel Publishing Co Inc.

Publisher:              Alan Giagnocavo
Project Editor:         Ayleen Stellhorn
Desktop Specialist:     Linda L. Eberly, Eberly Designs Inc.
Interior Photography:   W. F. Judt
Cover Photography:      W. F. Judt

ISBN # 1-56523-097-3

To order your copy of this book,
please send check or money order
for $19.95 plus $2.50 shipping to:
Fox Books
1970 Broad Street
East Petersburg, PA 17520

Manufactured in Korea

# DEDICATION

As a woodcarver I am aware that the talents I enjoy are gifts for which I must also be thankful. To be less than genuinely grateful is to deny these gifts and to rob oneself of a close relationship with the Giver of these gifts. So I offer thanks to God for what He has given me, endeavoring to be a good steward of these gifts.

I also wish to thank my wife Deborah for her unfailing support of my work over the last two decades and her willingness to make the sacrifices that are required of those who live with a self-employed artisan. Her faith in my "calling" as a woodcarver has been a tremendous blessing.

I want to thank Fox Chapel Publishing's Alan Giagnocavo for seeing the subject of this book as worthy of publication. Our collaboration on this project has been a happy experience.

Finally, much gratitude must be expressed to my many students over the years who have allowed me to learn as I teach. If the truth were known it would probably have to be said that I learned at least as much from them as they did from me.

*Boulders Page 48*

# TABLE OF CONTENTS

*Page 49*
*56*

# FOREWORD

When I was yet a novice carver, living in Ontario, I had occasion to hear of a retired carver in the area whose work had received numerous awards at the Canadian Nation Exhibition Carving Competition in Toronto, Canada. After obtaining his phone number, I arranged for a visit to this fellow's home.

After introducing ourselves, he led me through his house showing me the various carvings he had done, most of them in cedar and all of them delicate and technically challenging. Alongside his carvings were the ribbons he won at the various competitions he had entered over the years. I remember asking him about a family shield he had carved in relief, which was hanging prominently on a wall in the living room. "How did you do that?" I asked. With that question his manner became instantly bitter and indignant as he replied, "Those are my secrets that I worked years to develop, and I don't share them with anyone. They are going to the grave with me." Our meeting ended shortly thereafter.

His reply shocked me. It never occurred to me that woodcarvers might see their acquired skills as "trade secrets" to be hoarded, sold to the highest bidder or lost forever. Why would a hobbyist carver like this man, talented and experienced as he was, not wish to share the wealth of his experience with other carvers?

It seemed to me that this man was tormented by the misconception that giving away his knowledge and sharing his experience would somehow diminish him as a craftsman and as a person. Having invested time and energy developing his skills, he was not willing to part with them because they might allow some other carver to surpass him in ability. However, by default, this man isolated himself from the carving community. Not willing to give away his knowledge, he was also in no position to ask others to share the skills they had acquired through the same route of perseverance and ingenuity. Nothing would leave this man, and nothing could come in. He was alone with himself.

His demonstration of unrepentant selfishness has remained with me over 25 years, as an example of what I don't want to do. I don't want to become a miserly curmudgeon, hiding my gifts under a shroud of secrecy lest someone surpass my accomplishments and steal my glory.

There is a lake in Israel called the Dead Sea. It has the river Jordan flowing into it from the north, but no river flowing out. As a result, it is essentially a dead body of water. Nothing useful lives in it. However, the smaller sea to the north called Galilee receives water from the same Jordan river, but allows that water to flow out again from the south. This lake thrives and hosts many hundreds of species of marine life.

The carver who does not share what he knows with others eventually dies from the inside out. Unwilling to share, he puts himself in the position of being unable to ask for anything. Thus he cannot benefit from the experience of others which might lead him to new and exciting creative frontiers.

In my carving classes, in my writing, on the Internet and in seminars and workshops, I have resolved to do the opposite: to share what has been given to me, to enlighten others with my gifts (modest as they are, compared to some), and to bring into community those carvers who are suffering from isolation and loneliness.

I have discovered that when I freely give, I freely get. Not in the same meager measure, mind you, but overflowing, heaped up high, measure upon measure. There seems to be no bounds to the generosity of fellow carvers. I am humbled by it.

On the other hand, I find whenever I try to keep my gifts as a carver (and we all are gifted in some way) to myself, that is when the well starts drying up, the isolation starts setting in and self-doubt makes its assault on my soul. Many of you, I am sure, would concur with my findings.

It is in this spirit that this book is written. My goal is to help novice to advanced relief carvers by offering a wide collection of tips and techniques gathered over 25 years of carving in relief. To my knowledge, this has not been done before, leaving relief carvers with the task of finding these things out for themselves. Basic tasks such as laminating wood for relief panels, making your own relief carving bench and drawing relief patterns have not been addressed in other publications.

As I mentioned, I learned long ago that the best way to grow as a woodcarver was to share what I know with others. In order to share what I know, I had to first understand it well enough to express it in words and actions. So this book is an attempt to solidify my understanding of relief carving as much as it is to share my expertise with others.

—*Bill Judt*

# RELIEF CARVING TOOLS

## BASIC RELIEF CARVING TOOLS

For relief carving, mallet tools are essential. These are full-sized chisels and gouges in an assortment of sizes. They can be used with two hands or with one hand holding the tool and the other swinging a mallet.

I recommend a set of 12 mallet tools to start. To this set you can easily add single tools, and perhaps make a few more by converting less expensive carpenter tools into carving gouges and chisels. Most of my experienced carvers have about 25-30 tools in their collection.

In my carving studio, I have about 80 carving chisels and gouges. Many of these are duplicates, which I keep to help supplement the collections of my students; some are exotic tools that are used rarely; others are fragile antiques. But during the process of carving a typical relief, I use between 20 and 30 tools.

### Carver's tools versus carpenter's tools

Most people don't know the difference between carver's tools and carpenter's tools until they try to use a carpenter's chisel to do the work of a carving tool.

Carpenter's chisels have cutting edges that are shaped differently than carver's tools. They are flat on the underside, with a hollow ground (concave) slope on the top side that terminates at the cutting edge in a micro-bevel. They

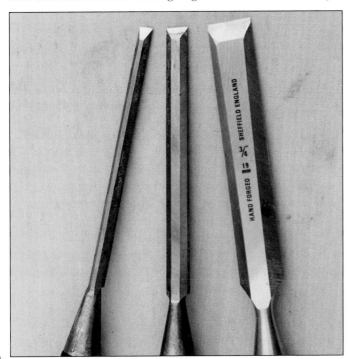

Carpenter's tools are designed to cut in a straight direction. They are flat on the underside, have a concave slope on the top, and end in a micro-bevel.

were designed to cut in a straight direction.

Carver's chisels have equal convex curves on both sides of the tool with no micro-bevel at the edge. Furthermore, carver's gouges have a convex curve on the underside and a micro-bevel that is placed on the top face of the

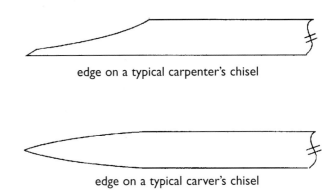

edge on a typical carpenter's chisel

edge on a typical carver's chisel

tool right at the cutting edge, to allow wood chips to curl away from the shank on the tool. (See "Properly shaped tool edge" on page 10.) Carver's chisels and gouges were designed to move freely in the wood and make curved cuts.

### Three additional home-made tools

Carpenter's tools are totally useless for woodcarving unless they are re-ground and re-shaped like carving tools. Carpenter's chisels are readily available at most hardware stores and are usually much less expensive than carving tools, so any carpenter's chisel that can be made into a carver's tool is money saved.

A typical set of carpenter's chisels contains $1/4"$, $1/2"$ and $5/8"$ chisels. The $1/4"$ and $1/2"$ chisels can be converted to shallow (#2 sweep) gouges with a "fishtail" shape, while the $5/8"$ chisel can be converted to either a shallow gouge or a skew chisel. There is a bit of grinding involved, and you'll want to be sure not to burn the steel, but converting a tool like this is not hard and should take only about 30 minutes.

Don't worry about the quality of steel in the carpenter's chisels. If they have "Sheffield" stamped on them, or if they produce a lively spark on the grinding wheel, they are probably made of good-enough quality steel.

I start by drawing on the chisels with a felt pen to indicate the metal that needs to be ground off the sides. I remove this excess metal and then grind the slope of the tool into a nice convex shape. (Look at the following picture to see how the chisels have been adapted for use as carving gouges/chisels.)

Carpenter's chisels can be reshaped to make excellent carving tools.

## Gathering together your collection of tools

Because each manufacturer includes different shapes and sizes of tools in a set, it is not possible to say exactly which tools you will need, but it is easy enough to generalize. Use the following list as a starting point.

#1-5mm (straight chisel)
#1-8mm (straight chisel)
#1s-8mm (skew chisel)
#1s-20mm (skew chisel made from 5/8" carpenter's chisel). This tool is useful to cut straight lines and level surfaces.
#2-8mm (very shallow gouge with fishtail shape made from 1/4" carpenter's chisel). This is a general purpose tool that is helpful in undercutting.
#2-12mm (very shallow gouge with fishtail shape made from 1/2" carpenter's chisel). This is a general purpose tool that is helpful in undercutting.
#3-5mm (very shallow gouge)
#3-20mm (very shallow gouge)
#5-8mm (shallow gouge)
#5-16mm (shallow gouge)
#7-12mm (medium tight gouge)
#9-10mm (tight gouge)

#9-15mm (tight gouge)
#11-2mm (very small veiner)
#11-3mm (small veiner)
#12-3mm (small 60° V-tool)
#12-6mm (medium 60° V-tool)
#13-8mm (medium 90° V-tool)

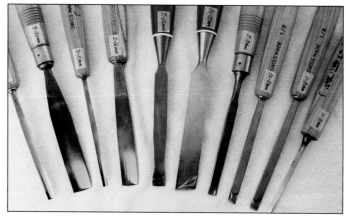

A collection of about 20 to 30 carving tools (above and below) will give you a good variety of tools for relief carving projects.

## Specialized tools

When you begin buying tools it is easy to get carried away. The urge to buy exotic tools—like the square-sided macaroni tools used for carving channels or the back-bent tools meant for carving beads in borders—is almost irresistible. However, these are tools that you should resist buying unless you need them for a special project.

Very large tools are of more use to the sculptor than the relief carver, unless the relief carver has a very large project to work on, such as a mural. Being most expensive of all, large tools should only be purchased on an "as-needed" basis.

Stay away from very small tools as well. Most veiners and V-tools under 3mm width are very hard to sharpen, even if you have a steady hand, good lighting and 20/20 vision.

Resist inexpensive tools, unless they happen also to be of very good quality. There are many sets of imported tools than sell for less than 25% of the retail price of the major brand name carving tools. Almost without exception, the steel and handles in these tools are vastly inferior. Their shapes are imprecise and they will not hold an edge no matter how you try.

Resist buying palm tools unless you need them for very fine detail, are working in softer woods and can sharpen them. Palm tools are made for carvers who hold the wood in one hand and the tool in the other. They are most useful to caricature carvers, bark carvers, golf-ball carvers and the like.

## Indicators of a quality tool

Quality tools are not hard to find these days. It used to be that there were very few quality lines of tools available in North America, but in the last decade European suppliers have extended their marketing to meet the demand of the rapidly growing North American carving market. One or two domestic brands are also showing up in the marketplace.

Quality tools can be defined as those that will last, even under daily use, to the third and fourth generation. In

This set of six chisels is available from Warren Cutlery.

Warren Cutlery also sells the Combi T4 kit.

Another choice from Warren Cutlery is the Combi TCE kit.

other words, if your tools will last long enough to be handed down to your great-grandchildren, then they are good-quality tools. Aside from this rather loose definition, there are definite signs to look for in a good tool.

Price is a reliable indicator. In the competitive market place manufacturers strive for the best quality at the lowest price. But there is a limit to how inexpensive a tool can be while still retaining quality. Most of the major tool manufacturers will sell their tools, either in sets or in open stock, for roughly the same price. Tools that are priced much higher than the standard for most brands are likely overpriced and will deliver no additional quality. Likewise, tools priced far below the average are almost always inferior in quality.

Next, look at the quality of the steel. A tool has to be hard enough to hold an edge and soft enough to keep from breaking when stressed by blows from a mallet or occasional prying. High carbon tools hold the best edges, better than most stainless steel tools, but the quality of edge attainable in stainless steel is more than adequate for carving purposes. For the average carver it is impossible to measure the carbon content of tools, so it is best to leave this to the manufacturer. Your best bet is to buy from a reputable dealer who will allow you to return a tool that is too hard, and therefore too fragile, or too soft to hold an edge.

Use this simple method to test the quality of steel in your tools. First, place the tool lightly on a grinding wheel. Observe the sparks that it produces. Next, place a common 6" spike against the same grinding wheel, using the same pressure, and observe the sparks. Finally, place a metal file against the wheel and observe the sparks that fly off the tool. The 6" spike will produce a few coarse, dull and lifeless sparks. A metal file (which is very hard steel with high carbon content) will produce a shower of sharp, lively sparks with even the lightest touch against a grinding wheel. A quality carving tool will produce a few less sparks than the metal file, and the sparks will not be quite as lively. But they will be far brighter, more abundant and much finer than the sparks produced by the common 6" spike.

Good handles are also important. I like handles which do not roll around on the work bench, as smooth round handles do. Ash, boxwood, rosewood and beech are commonly used for handles because these woods tend to stand up to the beating they take.

Consistent shape is also a consideration. The tool's metal must be even in thickness. If a tool has thin spots in some areas, it will be very hard to sharpen. V-tools and veiners are especially susceptible to inconsistencies in metal thickness. Unfortunately, it is hard to spot a tool with thin spots in the metal. These usually show up in the grinding process. If you discover a tool with this deficiency, by all means return it to your supplier for a replacement.

Stubai makes a full-sized (10") line, a Euro (8") line and a palm-sized (5") line.

A 10-piece mallet tool set is available from Falls Run Woodcarving Inc.

Stubai Woodcarving Tools from Austria are available in the United States from CJ Whillock.

# TOOL ACCESSORIES

Tools are like automobiles: they need accessories. These accessories are necessary to help you use, sharpen, carry and store your tools. Let's take a look at some of them.

### Tool rolls

Many commercial tool rolls are available, and many

Falls Run Woodcarving Inc. also sells a 6-piece mallet tool set.

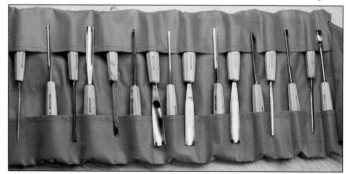

Alternating your tools blade-to-handle in a tool roll will prevent damage to the tools' edges.

carving sets come with them. If you are the type of carver who belongs to a club, or who carries tools with him on holidays or to workshops, then some tool carrying device is needed. You can buy a tool roll or you can make one. I like the tool rolls made out of canvas with an inside flap to protect the tool edges and a couple of long ties. Leather tool rolls are even better, but are more costly and harder to make. The pockets should be large enough to accommodate the largest tools you have.

### Wall-mounted tool racks

When you are finished carving for the day, you will need a place to store your tools so they are safely out of the way. Instead of sliding the tools into a tool roll each day, it is easier on you and the tool edges to place them each into their separate spots in a wall-mounted tool rack. There they will be safe from damage and not a threat to those, especially children, who might otherwise touch them.

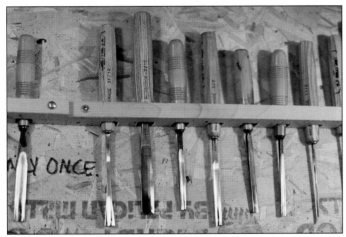

Wall-mounted tool racks are another way to safely store carving tools.

### Bench cloth

I do not like having my tools roll about the work bench as I carve, so I always lay them on a thick, folded piece of cloth placed on top of the table. This is the cheapest insurance policy you can get for protecting your tools. I lay the tools on the bench cloth in an orderly fashion, so that their sharp edges do not touch the metal of the neighboring tool. Some times it is best to place the tools so that they alternate handle-to-metal.

# STAMPING TOOLS

Stamping, sometimes called stippling, is a wonderful, easy-to-use and effective texture. Unfortunately, many carvers have never heard of it, and even fewer have ever used it. Yet stamping is an essential component in relief carving.

Stamping tools can be made with nothing more than a long steel bolt, a bench vise, a hacksaw and a 1/4" triangle file. Furthermore, they cost next to nothing and last a lifetime. Before I explain how to make a stamping tool, let me

Stamping tools add texture to areas of a relief carving off which light should not reflect.

first explain what a stamping tool looks like, what it does to the wood and where you can use the stamped texture in your carving.

## What is a stamping tool?

A stamping tool is basically a piece of steel, like a 1/4" x 6" or 3/8" x 6" bolt or piece of square steel stock,

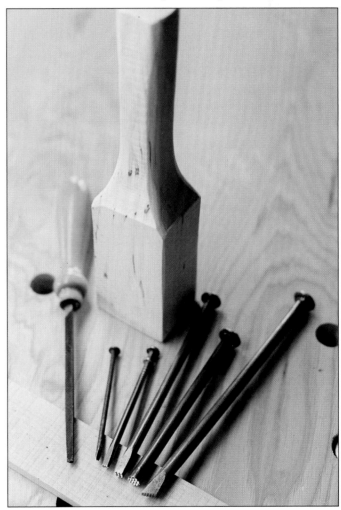

Bolts, nails and spikes are easily turned into stamping tools. A flat-sided mallet, made from scrap wood, is used to strike the stamping tools.

with a cross-hatch pattern of grooves filed onto its end. The grooves intersect at right angles to form sharp, even points. From the side these points look like little mountains separated by little valleys all in evenly spaced rows. The grooves are generally less than 1/16" deep and 1/16" apart.

A 1/4" bolt, for example, will have about three rows of valleys filed onto its end in each direction. This will produce four rows of points in each direction. This tool, when struck by a hammer or makeshift wooden mallet, will puncture wood, creating a pattern of holes over the wood surface. If the stamping tool is rotated in an oscillating motion, 1/16-turn on every stroke of the hammer or mallet, an even pattern of puncture marks will be created on the wood surface. You can achieve what I call a "saturated" stamping density by overlapping previously stamped areas with more stamping texture until none of the original smooth surface of the wood remains. The stamped texture, then, is a collection of densely packed holes on the surface of a piece of wood.

## What does stamping do for your carving?

A smooth, relief-carved surface is like a linoleum floor: shiny and slightly textured. Smooth, shiny surfaces reflect light. Stamping is to wood what carpet is to floor covering. It is a soft, unreflective surface, which upon close examination is anything but smooth. A stamped surface, like a carpet, does not reflect light. Rather, it absorbs light, appearing darker than the surrounding wood. Careful application of the stamped texture can add contrast and interest to your carvings.

But that is not all stamping does for your carving. I like to say that "stamping covers a multitude of carving sins." It helps you clean up areas of the background that are otherwise hard to carve cleanly. Stamping hides those pesky cuts left in the background of your relief by compressing the wood fibers so they close the wound. Stamping also helps to cover blemishes that result from grain that is too knurly to carve smoothly.

Stamping is usually the last thing you do to your relief carving before applying the finish. There are a few tricks to stamping, but it is generally simple to do. I have five stamping tools of different sizes. The small ones get into tight areas and the large ones cover more ground quickly. I even have a stamping tool with an angled contact surface that allows me to stamp in the areas that have been undercut.

## Where do I use stamping in my carving?

The most obvious place to use stamping is on the background of a relief carving. There it will do its best work of tidying up the background while providing contrasting texture and reflective values in relation to the objects in front of it. But I also use stamping around raised letters and around embossed (quilted-like) objects, like a repeating band of wolf footprints. On a number of wildfowl reliefs I have used stamping to texture bulrushes. Nothing makes a bulrush look more lifelike than stamping. Stamping also gives clothes, such as flannel shirts, a realistic texture.

**Stamping Tool Detail**

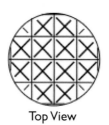

Top View

Side View

## How do I make a stamping tool?

Get a 1/4" x 6" or a 3/8" x 6" steel bolt from your local hardware store or some 1/4" or 3/8" square steel stock from a steel supplier. Just make sure the bolt has a flat, six-sided head. Round-topped bolts tend to destroy a wooden mallet easier and are also harder to control while striking them.

Large nails or spikes are also good for stamping tools. The metal in the nails is a little softer than the metal in the bolts and is easier to file. These are some suggestions:
1. 1/8" x 4" double-headed nail
2. 1/4" x 8" spike
3. 5/16" x 10" spike

Place the bolt, or whatever you've chosen, in a metal vise, and using a hacksaw, cut off the threaded portion of the bolt. Then use a fine flat file to flatten and square off the end of the bolt. It is important to start with a flat, smooth and square end before trying to file the grooves that make the points.

On a 1/4" bolt you would use a 1/4" triangle file to lightly file guidelines onto the bolt end. When you're finished, you'll want to have roughly three rows of "grooves" and four rows of "points." The grooves should be spaced about 1/16" apart.

Next, neatly file the grooves into the bolt end until they meet in sharp points about 1/16" high. Take care to file all the grooves in one direction before you file grooves at right angles to the first set. Be sure also to keep the triangle file from leaning over to one side or the other.

Finally, using one side of the triangle file, file the outside edges of the bolt or square stock to the same slope as the rest of the points. Remove any metal fragments from the stamping tool and try the tool on a scrap of wood.

## Common mistakes in making stamping tools

1. The grooves are too deep. This results in a coarse grid of points which will result in a crude and unattractive texture in the wood.

2. The grooves are crooked or unevenly spaced. This results in a noticeably uneven pattern when applying the tool to the wood. It also causes the points to misalign and enter the wood to uneven depths.

3. The stamping tool is too large. A large stamping tool, say $1/2$" or $5/8$" wide, theoretically should allow you to cover more area at a greater rate of speed when you stamp. But what happens in practice is that it takes far too much effort to make the points puncture the wood to their full depth. Usually a large stamping tool leaves a sickly looking pattern of shallow holes over the wood surface. It is very difficult to achieve a saturated texture with a tool that is too large.

## Common mistakes when applying stamping

1. Not driving the points to their full depth. This results in a shallow, sickly looking texture.

2. Not rotating the tool. Because the stamping tool has a cross-hatch grid pattern on its end, it is necessary to rotate the tool slightly with each blow of the hammer/mallet in order to create a random arrangement of holes in the wood. Otherwise the grid pattern of the tool shows up on the wood.

3. Not making enough holes to create a saturated texture. By saturated I mean that there are enough holes created by the stamping tool to eliminate any shine from the surface of the wood.

4. Stamping too much. Sometimes people stamp until the wood is pulverized. This looks ugly and should be avoided.

5. Missing areas that are under the undercuts.

6. Stamping too slowly. You should try to achieve about four hits of the hammer/mallet per second. That gets you into a rhythm that allows you to cover the area quickly and achieve a saturated density of holes. If you strike the stamping tool at a rate of one hit per second, it will take forever, and the quality of your stamping will deteriorate.

## What type of hammer/mallet should I use?

I never use my carving mallet to do my stamping. It is too valuable to be bruised and beaten on the end of a steel bolt. Instead, I use a home-made mallet that starts out as a 2" x 3" x 10" piece of birch hardwood. (See photo on page 5.) I cut the board to shape on my band saw so that I have a comfortable handle, and then soften the sharp edges with a stationary belt sander. This mallet is light, but its head is also wide enough to provide a good surface for striking the head of the bolt. Because it is wood, it does not

Mallets are simple to make. Covering the striking surface with string and glue increases the life of the mallet.

make as much noise as a steel hammer when I strike the stamping tool.

# MAKING A MALLET

Some people like to make things themselves. Others can't find what they want in a store or catalog, so they have to make it by themselves. Whatever your motivation, this section will help you make your own mallet.

I've never owned a store-bought mallet. This is mostly due to not being able to afford one when I started carving over twenty years ago, but it also has to do with the fact that I had a friend back then who had a lathe. Having a friend with a lathe is like having a friend who is a plumber, or a gardener, or an electrician — a handy fellow to have around.

## Basic requirements for a mallet

Every mallet needs to be:

**1. Inexpensive**

After all, the more you have to spend on a mallet, the less you have to spend on that special tool you've been eyeing on the tool store shelf for the last year. The mallet described in this section will cost you the wood it is made from and the cost of turning it to shape on a lathe.

**2. Long lasting**

Although mallets are not forever, they should last at least a few years. My favorite two mallets have been with

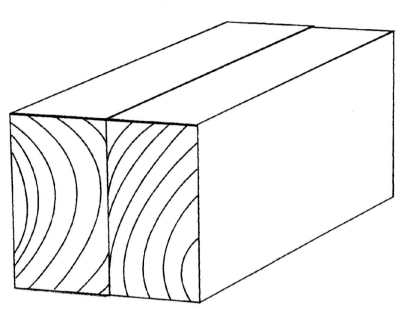

Laminate two 2" x 4" x 10"
boards for turning into mallet

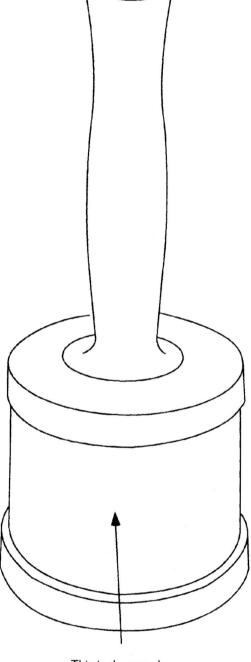

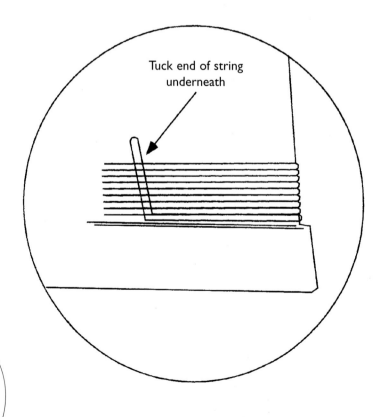

Tuck end of string
underneath

This is the way the
recessed area looks
before string is added

me for about five years now. My old, retired mallet has been pressed back into service by a friend who bought it from me for a "song." He tells me it's a great mallet, full of "experience."

### 3. Shaped to fit your hand

A mallet is like a pair of shoes. It has to fit or it is darned uncomfortable. An ill-fitting mallet will rub your hand to the point of blisters. A mallet that is too long will

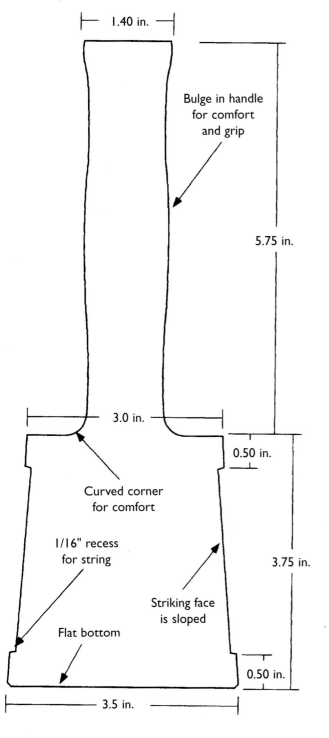

1.40 in.

Bulge in handle for comfort and grip

5.75 in.

3.0 in.

0.50 in.

Curved corner for comfort

1/16" recess for string

Striking face is sloped

3.75 in.

Flat bottom

0.50 in.

3.5 in.

strain your arm and wrist, and a mallet that is too short will not drive your tools hard enough.

### 4. The right weight

Your hand and arm are not the same as someone else's hand and arm. My hands, though strong and dexterous, are not very big and my wrists are quite thin, at least compared to the hands and wrists on the retired farmer who takes classes from me. His hands are massive and his wrists are like fence-posts. So it's easy to see why my mallet feels a little... well... "wimpy" to him. He prefers a mallet so big that I can hardly hold it in my hand and so heavy that my arm hurts just looking at it.

## Woods and weight

The fact is that a mallet which is even a little too heavy can strain your hand, arm and shoulder to the point where tendonitis begins. It's better to have two mallets: a heavy mallet for occasional use and a lighter mallet for general use.

For a light-weight mallet, I recommend the following woods: silver maple, alder, white birch, walnut and poplar. These woods are light but reasonably tough, especially the silver maple. For a medium-weight mallet I recommend the following woods: hard maple, yellow birch, western birch, cherry and beech. Of these, beech is probably the toughest because of its grain structure. It is the same wood used in wooden kitchen spoons. But the others in this selection will do a great job too.

For a heavy-weight mallet I recommend the following woods: lignum vitae, hickory, pecan and white oak. Of these, lignum vitae is most commonly used in commercially produced mallets and is the heaviest, but being a tropical wood it will check badly if left to dry. Hickory is incredibly tough, as is pecan. These are indigenous woods and will remain stable if properly seasoned. White oak is tougher than red oak, and heavier too.

For all of the above woods, find pieces that are full of curly, twisted grain; these pieces will be the toughest. Straight grain is somewhat weaker. Straight grain is like the fingers of your hand stretched out nice and straight. Twisted, knurly grain is like the fingers of both your hands knit together in a tight fist.

Note that there are no softwoods on this list. Softwoods will not stand up to the beating a mallet receives.

## Turning details

Prepare two 2" x 4" x 10" pieces of wood for laminating. If the boards are square and true, it will make the job of turning them much easier. I don't think it matters much which way you orient the growth rings in the two pieces. Use yellow carpenters glue and C-clamps to join the two, and let the glue dry overnight.

The drawing of the mallet template (left) indicates that the striking face on the mallet is sloped and recessed about 1/16". It is sloped to allow the mallet to strike the carving gouges at the correct angle. It is recessed to allow string to be wrapped around the mallet. Combined with glue, the string produces a tough, resilient and eventually replaceable striking surface for the mallet.

The base of the mallet head has a curved inside corner that is meant to provide a comfortable transition where the mallet moves from handle to head. Avoid sharp corners or beads in this area. The handle has a bulge in it to assist with the grip. The end of the handle is flared slightly to keep your hand from slipping off the mallet during heavy use.

There is a flat top on this mallet head. This allows the mallet to stand on its end on the worktable. This way it not only takes up little space, but it also keeps the mallet from rolling off the table when laid on its side.

Make sure the mallet is sanded smooth. The smoother it is, the more comfortable it will be in your hand. Do not apply any finish to the mallet yet. Wait until after the string and glue have been applied.

## Turning a lighter mallet

You can make a second mallet at the same time, this one a little narrower across the head. Instead of making it 3 1/2" tapering to 3", make the mallet 3" tapering to 2 1/2" across the width of the head. This will make a mallet that is nearly 30 percent lighter and especially suited to finer work. A lighter mallet will reduce the strain on your hand, wrist, elbow and shoulder, allowing you to work longer if needed, and certainly lessening the possibility of injury to your body.

## The striking surface

Once the mallet is turned you are ready to combine glue and string to create a tough membrane on the striking surface of the mallet. Butcher's string (the type that a butcher uses to wrap beef roasts) is best for this application. It will absorb the glue and is particularly tough and durable.

Start by winding the first few rows of string over an inch or so of string, as illustrated in the drawings. Enough glue needs to be applied to the wood surface to allow the string to stick to the wood as it is wound around the mallet. You do not have to apply glue to the whole mallet head at once. Apply glue to about one-third of the mallet head at a time. As the string is wound around the mallet, press the rows of string tightly together so there are no gaps.

When the mallet head has been completely wrapped with string, saturate the string with more glue. Work the glue into the string with your fingers until the string can hold no more. Then apply a thin layer over the top of the string as a top coat. When the glue and string are dry, sand the surface lightly to remove any rough ends of fiber and glue.

## Finishing the mallet

The mallet can be finished in many ways according to your preference. I simply apply a generous coat of hardwood floor paste wax to the exposed wood and buff it to a shine. The wax finish is very comfortable to the touch. There is no need to apply any finish to the stringed area.

Sooner or later the striking surface of the mallet will show wear and need to be replaced. This is as simple as cutting off the old string/glue and replacing it with a new layer. This way you can make your mallet last many years.

# SHARPENING

The best sharpening system is the simplest and the least expensive one. For this reason, I have resisted the temptation to buy expensive sharpening equipment and have made an effort to reduce my sharpening equipment to the minimum.

## Steps in sharpening

For the new tool, fresh out of the package, four steps are involved in sharpening. They involve first the grinding wheel; second, the bench stone; third, the slip stone; and fourth, the buffing wheel. If you are attempting to sharpen a tool that has been in use for a while, then follow only the last three steps.

Most tools come from the manufacturer with a "factory edge," an edge that is ground, honed and buffed on huge machines without the intervention of the human hand. These factory edges are characterized by a very sharp hollow ground surface on the underside of the tool, rather than the convex bevel found on carving chisels and gouges. Left as is, these tools will not move in and out of the wood

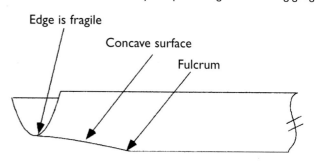

Factory-sharpened edge on a carving gouge

Edge is fragile
Concave surface
Fulcrum

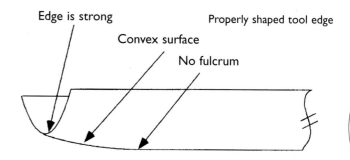

Edge is strong
Properly shaped tool edge
Convex surface
No fulcrum

smoothly. The heel of the tool becomes a fulcrum which kicks out the cutting edge from the wood. Factory edges must be re-ground so they have a gentle, even, convex curve, leading to a sharp, but not too thin or fragile, edge.

I always test each tool as it comes from a supplier to see if it will move through the wood easily. If not, which is most often the case, I take it to the grinding wheel and start the sharpening process.

A grinder gives a new store-bought tool its general shape.

## Grinding wheel

Grinding wheels always rotate into the tool edge. Only use a grinding wheel to impose a general shape on the tool edge. Carving tools need only be taken to the grinding wheel when they are new from the supplier, when they have been chipped on the cutting edge or when the tools edge has been rounded off from repeated buffing over a period of time.

The strategy is to remove the least amount of metal possible, thus extending the useful life of the tool. My heavily used tools go back to the grinding wheel only once or twice each year, and this is usually because repeated buffing has rounded the edges, making them blunt. My other tools might never go back to the grinding wheel after their initial shaping.

Grinding wheels come in various shapes, sizes, grits, compounds and capabilities. I have used the common carborundum wheel (1" x 6" x 1725 rpm), and also the "cool white" aluminum oxide wheels. The white wheels are a bit more forgiving, as they do not heat up the tool edge as quickly. I avoid tool rests, preferring to rest my hand on the motor and using muscle memory (see page 13, "Muscle Memory") to guide the tool.

My grinding wheel rotates at 1725 rpm. This is the fastest speed I recommend. If you can gear the speed down, even better. I use old furnace or old washing machine motors, to which I fasten a work arbor (see page 22, "Grinding /Buffing Center"), which holds the grinding wheel. This apparatus is very simple, efficient and inex-

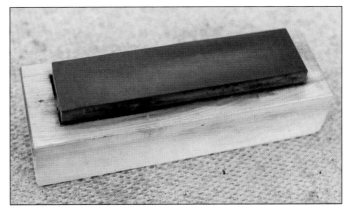

A bench stone smoothes away the marks left by the grinder.

pensive. Once I have shaped the tool on the grinding wheel, I move to the bench stone to refine the shape.

## Bench stone

The bench stone is used to smooth out the course grinding marks left on the carving tool by the grinding wheel. I use an India Oil Stone (90x/600x Aluminum Oxide Oil Stone). These stones are durable and cost very little, but must be used with a light oil lubricant. (See page 16, "Other Sharpening Hints.") Carborundum bench stones are good too, but they tend to wear more rapidly than the India Stone. I use the 600x side of the stone to hone the tool.

I made a wooden box to hold my bench stone and place the box/stone in one of the vises on my work bench. This allows me to use the stone vigorously without it slipping. The box also retains some of the oil that is applied to the stone and will keep the stone from drying out.

The purpose of the bench stone is to refine the shape of the tool edge, so that the bevel on the underside is even and gentle, and to produce a noticeable "wire-edge" on the tool. This wire-edge must run the full width of the tool-edge, indicating that you have shaped the underside of the tool completely to the edge.

The wire-edge can be felt better than it can be seen. Wipe the oil off the tool and drag your finger on the tool's inside face. You should be able to feel a wire-edge, or burr. Test the edge of the tool by lightly dragging the edge across your thumbnail. You will notice that the edge is quite rough. But it will drag far less than it did when it came off the grinding wheel. Once you are satisfied that this wire-edge is adequate, you are ready to move to the slip stone.

## Slip stones

Slip stones are usually much finer than bench stones. They come in smaller sizes that allow you to use them with one hand holding the slip stone and the other hand holding the carving tool. My slip stones are made of white and black "Arkansas," a natural quarried stone that is very fine.

Slip stones are used to erode the wire-edge left on the

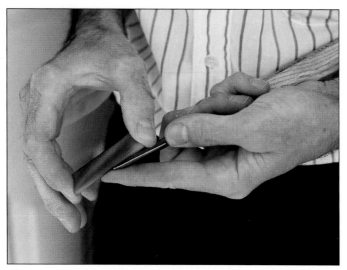
Slip stones form a micro-bevel on the tool's edge.

surfaces of the tool. I use a thin wedge-shaped slip stone for this. Otherwise, I use a slip stone with edges that are angled and more blunt.

Test the edge of the tool by lightly dragging the edge across your thumbnail. You will feel a slight drag from the tool. But it will drag far less than it did when it came off the bench stone. When the wire-edge has been removed, you are ready to move to the buffing wheel.

### Buffing Wheel

Once you have removed the wire-edge from the tool, you are ready to buff the edge of the tool to a razor-sharp edge. Slip stones leave the edge much smoother than bench stones, but under a microscope you would see that the edge is still far too rough to leave a polished cut in hardwood.

Buffing/honing compounds contain abrasives, mixed with wax, that are much finer than slip stones and polish steel to a much higher degree. Buffing compounds come in a huge assortment of colors and properties. Generally, you can rely on "green" compound (Tripoli: chromium oxide mixed with other fine abrasives and a bonding compound) and "white" compounds (stainless) to work quite nicely.

Buffing wheels always rotate off the tool edge. You must apply moderate pressure on the tool against the buffing wheel in order to buff effectively. If you are applying enough pressure to stall the motor ($1/4$HP, 1725rpm) then you are pressing too hard.

A mistake most people make is to round off their tool edge at the buffing stage. Your tool edge should touch the buffing wheel at the tangent or a couple of millimeters ($1/16$") below the tangent under pressure. Any lower than this and the buffing wheel will start rounding off the otherwise crisp angle of the tool edge. You do not want the curve of the bevel on the underside of the tool to change angles as it approaches the edge. The underside of the tool should end up being a consistent arc from heel to cutting edge.

Buffing occurs on both faces of the tool: top side and underside. The underside receives the lion's share of the buffing, but buffing the inside edge will polish the micro-bevel that was placed on the tool edge during the slip

tool by the bench stone. You slide the slip stone across and into the inside edge first, about 20 strokes, and then flip the tool over and do the same to the outside edge, about 10 strokes. Stroke the inside and outside edges of the tool repeatedly until you can no longer detect even the slightest wire-edge on both sides of the tool. As the slip stone wears the wire-edge on the inside face of the tool, it will form what is called a "micro bevel" on the inside face. This micro bevel is very narrow and allows the wood to curl at the tool edge as the tool moves through the wood.

Care must be taken to avoid rounding off the tool edge during this process. Keep the slip stones positioned at the edge of the tool at the lowest angle possible that still allows you to erode the wire-edge. This will take some experimentation and practice, but is a skill worth mastering.

Some tools, such as the V-tool and the small veiner, require a thin slip stone that will reach into the restricted

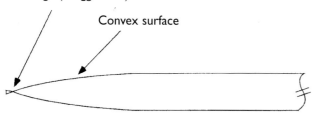
Chisel edge before using slip stone
Wire edge (exaggerated)
Convex surface

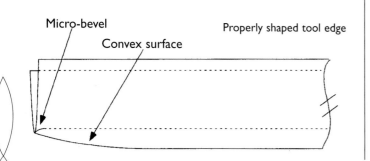
Micro-bevel
Convex surface
Properly shaped tool edge

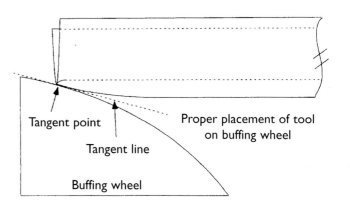
Tangent point
Tangent line
Proper placement of tool on buffing wheel
Buffing wheel

stone stage. During buffing, test the edge of the tool by lightly dragging the edge across your thumbnail. There will be no perceptible drag from the tool. Instead, a sharp tool will slip across your thumbnail effortlessly.

## Using "muscle memory" to keep edges sharp

"Muscle memory" can be defined as the ability of muscles to "remember" a certain position, grip and movement. Muscle memory is the best alternative to jigs and automated sharpening devices. It costs nothing but time and practice. It is very flexible, reliable and portable. It will eventually allow you to sharpen your carving tools far faster and better than any jig on the market.

Think of the muscle memory involved in riding a bike. Your muscles, along with your eyes and the balance center in your brain are all coordinating to allow you to pedal, balance, move your legs, steer, lean into turns and manipulate gears and brakes. It takes some time to learn the skill of bike riding, but eventually it becomes automatic. It also becomes a skill that you do not forget.

Position your grinding wheel, bench stone and buffing wheel so you can comfortably use them at the same height and angle every time. You must find a comfortable, firm and reliable grip for your tools as you use each of your grinding, shaping and buffing tools.

It is better to keep your arms close to your body rather than to extend your arms when sharpening and buffing. The closer your arms are to your body, the more control you will have over them. It is also useful to rest your hand on the grinding wheel motor so your hand can become a substitute tool rest/guide.

After sharpening a few tools you will already have a sense of what it feels like to position, grip and move your tools across the surfaces of  grinding wheels, honing wheels and buffing wheels. Soon your muscles will "remember" what they are to do without you telling them directly, and you will be on your way to achieving muscle memory. If you learn this single skill you will have learned the most important skill in sharpening your tools.

## Preventing tool damage

Tools can be damaged any number of ways, but the most common are the following:

### Burning on the grinding wheel

During the initial stages of sharpening a tool, it is very easy to "burn" the edge of a tool on the grinding wheel. A burnt edge is one that has turned dark blue or black from excessive heat generated by pressing the tool too hard and too long against the grinding wheel, without quenching the tool in cool water. A burnt edge has lost its temper, which means it has lost its hardness, and will not hold a sharp edge for long.

Grinding must always be a matter of alternately removing small amounts of metal and quickly cooling the tool edge in water. It is important that your grinding wheel be mounted to a motor that runs 1725rpm or less. Higher speeds than this generate too much heat too quickly and make it very hard to avoid burning the tool edge. Keep a small plastic container of water near your grinding wheel for quenching the tool. Metal containers are hard and will damage the edge of any tool that inadvertently touches the sides of the containers.

If you accidentally "burn" a tool edge, you can grind away the affected metal and start again in an area of the tool that has not lost its temper. When I burn an edge, I generally continue with the rest of the sharpening process and rely on subsequent sharpenings to eventually remove the weakened area.

### Dropping

Sooner or later you will drop a tool onto the floor. Murphy's Law determines that the tool will not land handle down, nor will it drop onto the soft rubber mat you placed below your feet. It will drop edge down and contact concrete or metal, thus damaging the tool edge.

If a tool does drop, let it fall rather than trying to catch it. Better to repair a chipped edge than have to go to the hospital for stitches. And be sure to get your feet out of the way of the falling tool! I speak from experience here, and often show my students the 1" cut I inflicted on myself as a result of trying to catch a tool that was in the process of dropping.

### Touching another piece of metal

All it takes to dull a tool edge is to allow it to touch another piece of metal or glass. If a tool edge touches a vise, a ceramic coffee cup or another tool, it will suffer damage. You will need to develop good tool-handling habits. Most damage occurs when tools are placed back onto the table carelessly. I have seen some of my carving students actually drop their tools on top of others in their haste to grab another tool.

### Carving in abrasive wood

Some woods contain amounts of very fine sand which can quickly wear the edge of a sharp tool. How the sand gets into the wood is not important, but woods like teak are full of sand. Some mahoganies have similar properties. You might want to investigate the abrasive properties of your favorite carving wood if your tools are dulling more quickly than you would expect. Dirty wood will also cause damage to your tools. Avoid using any wood that has lain in sand or dirt.

### Prying with the tool

When a chip of wood will not release from the carving, some carvers resort to prying it out rather than cutting it out. This occurs most often in corners and tight spaces. Sharp tool edges are not meant for prying and will sometimes break. Always push the tool through the wood completely, or in the case of restricted corners, ensure that wood is cut out rather than ripped out.

### Squeezing the tool into a restricted area

V-tools are particularly susceptible to breaking when they are pushed into tight spaces. The wings of a V-tool are easily squeezed together causing the metal to break at the bottom of the "V." Damage is often severe and can result in losing as much as 1/2" of the length of the tool. When using a V-tool (or any tight gouge) in a restricted area, make sure both wings of the V-tool (or both shoulders of the gouge) are out of the wood. Only part of the tool should be in the wood at a time.

### Rust

Corrosion is another cause of tool damage. In the worst case, the surface metal of a tool becomes badly pitted, making it unattractive and somewhat difficult to sharpen. Rust occurs more often in places close to the ocean, but it can also occur as a result of a person's body chemistry. Some people have sweaty hands that deposit salt onto their tools. In cases such as this, I recommend stainless steel tools. These will not rust.

## Knowing when your tools are dull

You will know your tools are dull when they become hard to push through the wood or when they leave a scratchy surface rather than a polished cut. The scratches left behind are tracer lines. There will be a tracer line for every nick or blemish on the tool edge, no matter how small that nick is. Unless the tool-cut is dark and shiny in relation to the surrounding un-carved wood, the tool is likely in need of sharpening.

### Thumb test

The thumb test is one indicator of a dull tool. When you drag the cutting edge of a dull tool across your thumbnail, it will drag. A tool with a chipped edge will feel ragged. But a very sharp tool can barely be felt as it passes over the thumbnail. There is virtually no friction at all. A truly sharp edge cannot be seen with the naked eye, but

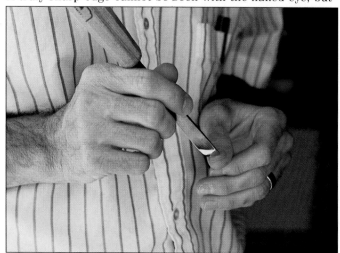

A razor-sharp tool will slip effortlessly across your thumbnail.

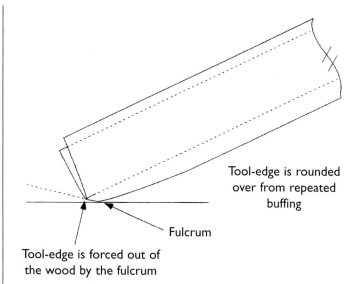

Tool-edge is rounded over from repeated buffing

Fulcrum

Tool-edge is forced out of the wood by the fulcrum

in a strong light one can sometimes see nicks and blemishes on the edge of a tool that is damaged.

### Tools that skip out of the wood

Another indicator of a dull tool is the tendency of the tool to skip out of the wood. Even if the edge is freshly buffed, the tool might refuse to stay in the wood, making it difficult, if not impossible, to make long, un-interrupted cuts.

If you have to raise the tool handle high to get the tool's edge to enter the wood, it is likely that the edge is rounded off. If the tool skips out of the wood as you lower the handle in order to push the tool forward through the wood, it is a clear sign that the edge has been rounded off and become blunt from repeated buffing. The thumb test will not reveal this fault because the edge may not contain any nicks or blemishes. Only pushing the tool through the

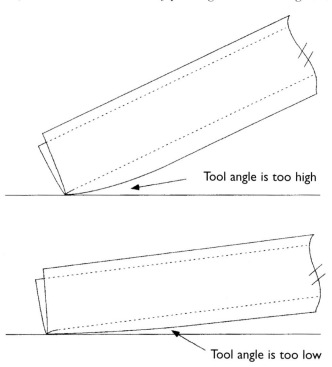

Tool angle is too high

Tool angle is too low

wood will show whether the tool needs to be reshaped at the cutting edge.

## Shaping your tools

The smaller the angle of the cutting edge of a tool, the lower its handle will be to the wood when you carve. This will make it easy to push the tool through the wood because most of the force from your hand and arm is directed forward rather than down. But it might result in scraped knuckles and a loss of the tool's mobility. The greater the angle of the cutting edge, the higher the tool's handle will have to be before the tool's edge enters the wood. It will also require more effort to move the tool through the wood. This is because more of the force from your hand and arm is directed downward and less is directed forward. The proper angle for the cutting edge of a tool is measured less in degrees than it is measured by the ability of your knuckles to clear the wood and the force that is required to move a sharp tool through the wood.

### Multiple facets/fulcrums

An inexperienced carver might not realize that he has

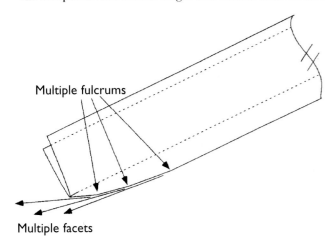

Multiple fulcrums

Multiple facets

shaped his tools so that the bevel on the underside of the tool is actually a collection of facets. A facet is one flat surface adjoining another flat surface at a slightly different angle, like the facets of a diamond. The problem with every facet is that it has a corner on each side. Corners act like fulcrums to push the tool edge out of the wood as the tool is pushed forward and must be rounded off so they form a continuous curve based on an arc.

## Shapes and angles of tool edges

When sharpening tools for my students, I often come across tools shaped rather oddly, with shoulders on a gouge ground way back, for instance, or the wings of a V-tool protruding way ahead. Unless there is a specific reason to have tools shaped this way, I try to persuade my students to shape their tools for the best all around performance.

## V-tools

V-tools can be shaped so that the wings of the tool are:
• leading the bottom of the "V" (angled greater than 90°)

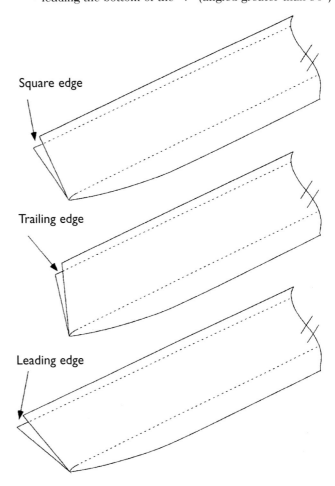

Square edge

Trailing edge

Leading edge

• trailing the bottom of the "V" (angled less than 90°)
• square (at 90°) in relation to the shaft of the tool.

There are advantages to each shape. The leading edge permits the most efficient angle for cutting through the wood. The wings, leaning forward as they do, cut the top surface of the wood before the bottom of the "V" starts cutting, preventing the wood from chipping on the surface. In addition, the angle of the cutting edge is great enough to offer the advantage of a slicing action as the tool moves through the wood. The tool will cut easily and cleanly, except when it arrives at a vertical wall, where it cannot help but leave the uncut wood fibers at the bottom of the "V" uncut.

The trailing edge allows the V-tool to cut right up to a vertical wall, without leaving any fibers at the bottom of the "V" uncut. But at all other times, the bottom of the "V" is cutting deep in the wood before the wings can cut the surface of the wood. This can cause chipping and ripping of the wood, and will definitely make the tool harder to push through the wood.

The square edge is a compromise between the other two shapes, and will offer you the most advantages and the least disadvantages. It will leave only a few fibers uncut at the bottom of the "V," but will cut quite easily and cleanly through the wood.

### Skews

Skews arrive in your shop from the factory with as much as a 45° angle ground on the cutting edge. This makes the skew useful for getting into tight corners, but almost useless for anything else. In order for the skew to still access tight corners while also being useful as a lev-

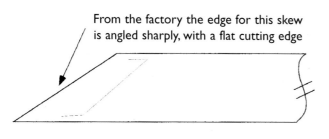

From the factory the edge for this skew is angled sharply, with a flat cutting edge

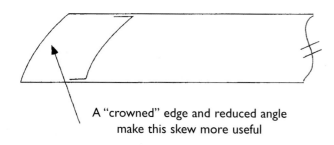

A "crowned" edge and reduced angle make this skew more useful

eling, lettering and straight-line tool, the angle of the cutting edge must be reduced to about 20°.

The face of the cutting edge should have a slight crown to it, rather than being flat. This will allow the tool to move more easily through the wood when leveling a surface without the shoulders becoming buried in the wood.

In special circumstances, you may need a 45° skew, but for general use a skew should have an angle of about 20°.

### Gouges

Gouges can also be shaped so that their shoulders are swept forward or backward from the bottom of the cutting edge for the same reason as the v-tool. The best compromise between access and sharp cutting is to have the shoulders even with the bottom of the cutting edge.

### Straight chisels

These tools should have a cutting edge of 90° to the length of the tool, but with a slight crown similar to the skew chisel illustrated earlier.

## Other sharpening hints

### Oilstones vs. water stones

I prefer oilstones over water stones. Oilstones are less messy than having water from a water stone splashing over wooden benches and mixing with steel cuttings.

Oilstones wear far less than water stones, because they are made of harder material, and they are generally less expensive too. I also prefer oil slip stones to water slip stones. The slips made of Arkansas stone can last a lifetime and retain their shape.

Oilstones do not need expensive honing oil, although the sometimes-expensive commercial honing oils are good products. Automatic transmission fluid, the red-colored stuff you put into your car's automatic transmission, is a wonderful lubricant and is priced at one-tenth the cost of honing oils. This oil does not clog the pores of the stones and allows you to wipe the stone completely clean with a dry rag. It also does not present any risk of spontaneous combustion.

### Diamond bench stones

There is not much to say about these except that they are expensive, work well, stay flat longer and require no lubricant. An occasional washing with water seems to do the trick.

## A WORD ABOUT POWER TOOLS

I do not use hand-held power tools for relief carving for a number of reasons: I find them under-powered, too heavy, inaccurate, limited in their control and expensive. The only exception to this statement is the hand-held plunge-type router that is pictured later in the book. Most importantly, I feel power tools are a poor substitute to trained hands holding a sharp, well-chosen gouge and a mallet. Power tools become less effective the larger the relief carving becomes.

## MACHINE RECOMMENDATIONS

Not many of us can afford to be like "Tim the Tool Man," picking up every tool available regardless of price. So we have to make choices, especially in the area of power equipment. Not only is cost a major factor, but space has to be considered, too. There are machines that have limited usefulness to a relief carver, and others that are essential. Here are some suggestions for tools to accept or reject for your carving shop.

### Table saw

I have a real nice craftsman 10", 1HP, 220V, solid steel, floor-standing table saw that gets used "once in a blue moon."

Mostly it is used as a table upon which I place other tools, pieces of wood, bags and boxes. When it does get used as a saw it is almost never for anything related to wood carving. I do not use it to rip boards to width because the band-saw is far quicker and more efficient. I do not use it to cross-cut lumber because the radial arm saw does that better. I do not use it for sanding, or molding or dadoing or mitering. I have dedicated tools that do each of these better.

### Jointer

A jointer is an essential shop tool. It is used to prepare boards for lamination.

Here is an absolutely essential piece of equipment. You cannot begin to surface boards in preparation for planing or edge boards for lamination without this tool.

Be prepared to search around for a good used unit if you wish to save money. Most often, jointers are purchased by would-be cabinet makers who rarely get to use them.

Your jointer should have a fixed out-feed table with easily adjustable cutter blades. The in-feed table should be adjustable. Look underneath the in-feed table to see if it can be accurately set with adjustment screws.

Jointers that come with wedge-shaped slides upon which the in-feed and out-feed tables glide are not as accurate as the jointer described above. Higher-priced models of this type may have enough precision built into the jointer castings to keep them accurate.

The jointer I use is a Craftsman 6" floor-standing model, about 15 years old. It has a separate motor and is belt driven. I like the way the cutter head adjusters allow me to set the height of the blades to exactly match the height of the out-feed table, allowing the out-feed table to remain fixed. With this jointer I can produce joints that are 99% perfect. When glued together and subsequently carved, these joints are nearly invisible.

### Band saw

A band saw is necessary to cut the perimeter of the relief panel and to rip boards.

You will need a band saw to cut the perimeter of the carving to shape. You will also use it to rip boards to widths narrow enough to fit your jointer and to cut small pieces for repairing mistakes in your carving. In short, you will use it with every carving you do.

I use a 14" Rockwell floor model band saw, with a 1/2" 8tpi blade. This machine is stable, easily adjusted, powerful and accurate. Once it is fine-tuned, it will operate maintenance-free for a year at a time. The throat of this model is wide enough for most jobs.

I added a table extension to my band saw, which enables me to handle wide panels easily. This band saw has pre-drilled holes in the table top to allow me to fasten angle-iron to it on so that the table can be extended. A dust collection system can be attached to this machine to help keep the shop tidy and safe.

Avoid the three-wheel band saws. These are intended for the hobbyist and are both under-powered and too inaccurate for working in two-inch-thick hardwoods.

## Router

My router is a 2hp Makita plunge router. It has enough power for working in hardwoods, and its plunge capability is essential. These machines are sturdy enough to last for decades, but are priced so that they are within reach of the hobbyist. I had to purchase my bits separately, opting for $1/4$", $5/16$" and $3/8$" straight bits with carbide tips. The Vermont American line of router bits are good quality and affordable bits that will last through the routering of many relief panels.

## Radial Arm Saw

Radial arm saws are used in relief carving to cross-cut lumber and are handy for many other non-relief projects.

You will need a tool like this to cross-cut your lumber to length. Aside from this you will likely not use this tool for relief carving. But it is a useful saw for many other non-carving projects and will justify its purchase quickly. A used radial arm saw is most often a good buy. Mine is a 10" Craftsman, to which I quickly added side tables for handling lumber up to ten feet long. Take time to adjust this saw so that it delivers square cuts every time, following the instructions in the manual.

## Planer

A planer is used to cut pieces of lumber to the same thickness in preparation for laminating into larger panels. A jointer must first be used to accurately surface one side of a board. That surface is placed down against the planer

A planer is used to cut boards to the same thickness.

table and fed into the cutters which are above the board. The cutters, being parallel to the planed table, cut the second surface of the board completely parallel to the first. You cannot easily machine boards to thickness without this tool.

# ODDS AND ENDS

You will also want to consider the following small tools to make relief carving a little easier.

## Bar/Pipe clamps

Although these come in many shapes and forms, I use the simple pipe clamps because they are inexpensive and available locally. The pipe needs to be purchased separately from the clamp head and foot, and it needs to be threaded as well. Although plumbing shops can thread the pipe, it is becoming easier to find threaded pipe at the same place you purchase the attachments.

Most of my pipe clamps are between three- and four-feet long. I have some that are eight-feet long, but I use these only rarely. Some of my pipe clamps use $3/4$" pipes; others use 1" pipe. The thicker pipe is stronger and will last longer.

## C-clamps

You will need between six and ten C-clamps to hold the wood in place as you laminate your relief panels. If you use four boards to build a relief panel, then there will be three joints requiring a total of six C-clamps to align the boards and keep them from separating while being clamped in the pipe clamps. If you have six boards in a panel, then ten clamps are required. C-clamps are better than spring loaded A-Clamps for holding boards in alignment.

## Bench dogs

Wooden bench dogs will inflict less damage on your relief carving panels.

A friend turned some wooden bench dogs for holding my relief panels on top of my work tables and since then I have not used my more expensive brass dogs. Wooden dogs do less damage to the edge of your panel, cost less, are warm and comfortable to the touch and less likely to damage a router bit that exits the edge of the panel. My wooden dogs were turned out of scrap hard maple to fit a 5/8" hole. They have one face that is flat, but angled slightly, so that they grab the panel securely.

## Rubber floor mats

Standing on a concrete floor is hard on the feet and the legs. If at all possible, purchase a good quality floor mat to provide some cushion while you stand. Your feet will thank you for it.

## Vacuum cleaner

A small shop vacuum is needed for a long list of small tasks in the shop, not the least of which is sucking up the wood chips from the surface of your relief. Keep in mind that a shop vacuum is not a substitute for a dust collec-tion system. Should you need to control dust, consider either a good quality dust mask or a commercial vacuum system to gather the dust from power equipment.

Generally speaking, relief carving produces dust only during the sawing, planing and jointing process of assembling a relief panel and during the routering stage. The rest of the time, relief carving is relatively dust free.

## Shop lighting for relief carving

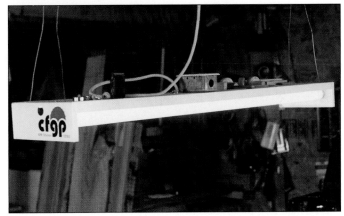

A fluorescent lighting fixture that can be raised and lowered reduces or increases shadows depending on your preference.

I like to have adjustable hanging fluorescent lights close to my carving table. These tube lights cast a four-foot-wide swath of light over the work bench and allow me to carve without always working in the shadow of my hands and body.

My workbench is located close to the windows so when I carve during the day, natural light streams across my carving from one side. The fluorescent lights on the other side of my work bench (two tubes of 40 watts each), help eliminate the dark shadows cast by the strong light from the window. With light from both sides, I can usually see what I am doing.

My fluorescent lights are suspended from the ceiling by a simple system of ropes and pulleys. I can raise or lower them as I wish for optimum lighting. During the last stages of finish tool marking, I like the lights hanging low because they cast sharper shadows and allow me to see the tool markings clearly. For the times I wish to work in the deeper areas of the carving, I raise the fluorescent lights so that I can see down into the tight spaces at the lowest levels. The fact that these lights raise and lower also makes it easy to raise them out of the way when you wish to move large pieces of lumber or plywood around.

# LIGHT TABLE PLANS
## Why a light table?

Most carvers eventually want to create unique carvings. Perhaps the carving designs that everyone else uses just don't have the same appeal they used to. Perhaps a special occasion has come along that demands something

A light table provides the perfect surface on which to design patterns.

different. Or maybe the carver has been asked to do a commission with a specific theme and design. Whatever the impetus, sooner or later most carvers are going to need to do some design work in preparation for that special carving project.

## What is a light table?

A light table is just the sort of special drawing center that every serious carver needs. The light table provides you with the space you need to draw comfortably. But more than that, it provides you with light to make your drawing easier and quicker. The light comes from below rather than above, shining through layers of paper as you trace, draw and rearrange your design.

A light table provides a large surface on which to work. There is room for pencils, paper, compasses, pantographs, photographs, rulers and the like. The living room coffee table, already crowded with books, newspapers and the latest in decorator candles just won't do. Neither will the kitchen table, because of the time restraints placed on its use.

Light tables come in various sizes. My main table is custom-built and is the basis for the light table pattern I have included in this article.

My father-in-law built my main light table for me as a Christmas gift many years ago. I had to strap it to the roof of my old Dodge Caravan and haul it across two Canadian provinces to take it home. It arrived safely and has been in active service now for about ten years. It is 54" long by 42" wide by 12" thick and provides me with ample room to draw the larger patterns that I use for my carvings.

My other light table is a government surplus table, bought for a song and built like a battleship. It gets used mostly by my students and features an arborite cutting surface off to the side of a smaller light box. It also has a set of drawers for storing things.

## Uses for a light table

1. I use a light table to trace photographs and artwork to produce the pencil-line drawings that I incorporate into my carving patterns. I can, for example, take a photo of my subject (say it's a building, a person, or an animal), tape the photo onto the light table with masking tape (don't use other tapes) and trace a pencil-line drawing of it in minutes. This pencil-line drawing can then be edited, scaled and manipulated until it is suitable for use in my pattern.

2. I sometimes also use the light table with the light off. Let's say I have to draw something original, that is, without tracing. The best way to do this is with the light off. The large working surface of the light table is still at my disposal and the glass surface is smooth and hard, allowing clean and accurate drawings. Tape adheres well to it too, and the glass surface can be cleaned with window cleaner.

3. Once I have an image on paper, I can use a pantograph to scale it larger or smaller, a compass to draw circles and a ruler to measure and align the components. This is all done easily on the light table's large and flat surface. I even have space for the required coffee cup to rest safely out of arm's reach.

4. Once I have traced or drawn the various components of a design and scaled them to their correct sizes, I illuminate the light table and arrange these components into their proper positions relative to each other and to the boundaries of my pattern. I do this by layering the various parts and taping them into position. On top of them, I lay another piece of paper onto which I have drawn the borders for the final design. Then I trace the arranged components to create a complete, properly scaled pattern on a single large sheet of paper.

## Construction considerations

Here are the basic building requirements for a light table to ensure it will be a safe and effective workstation for your carving shop.

### The glass top

1. Choose a smooth glass top, made from $5/16$" tempered glass. Tempered glass is stronger and safer to use. The edges of the glass should be sanded smooth so that when you handle the glass (during installation and for cleaning) you do not cut yourself. Even though the glass is tempered, do not use the glass top as a cutting surface. Sharp blades of any kind can scratch the surface and make it less suitable for drawing.

2. The glass should be inset into the edges of the table box so that it lies flush with the top edge of the box. That way you can move your ruler and drawing tools around the glass top without them catching the edge of the box.

3. There should be two or three narrow ($3/4$") lengthwise supports placed directly under the glass for support. In addition to the inset edges of the light table box, these supports will keep the glass from breaking under weight and allow you to lean on the table top as you work.

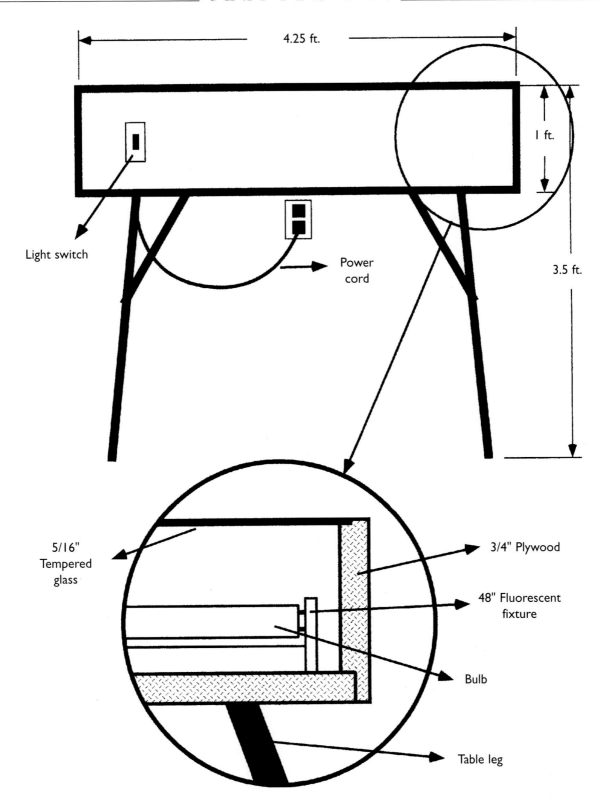

4.25 ft.

1 ft.

3.5 ft.

Light switch

Power cord

5/16" Tempered glass

3/4" Plywood

48" Fluorescent fixture

Bulb

Table leg

Light table, front view

4. Be sure the glass top is easily removable for cleaning. This means that it should not be fit too tightly into the top of the light table box.

5. Stay away from plastic tops. They scratch too easily and are usually more expensive than glass.

**The plywood box body**

1. Build the box with sturdy 3/4" plywood. Use screws instead of nails, and fit some supports into the corners to facilitate assembly of the box.

2. Cut grooves around the inside of the top edge of the

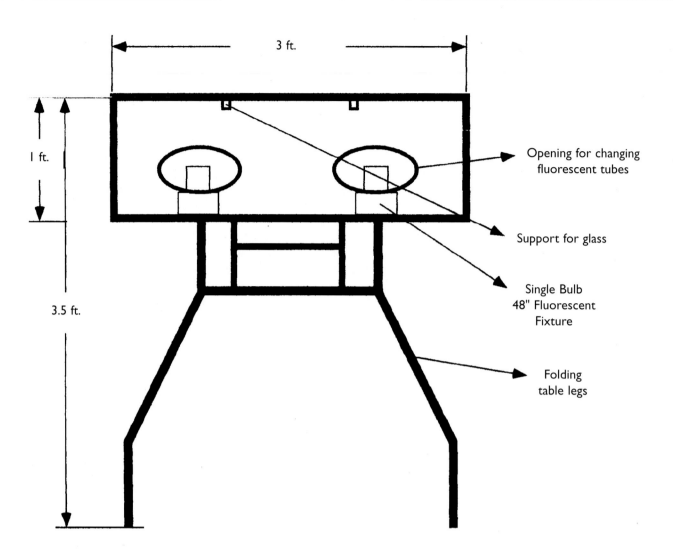

3 ft.

1 ft.

3.5 ft.

Opening for changing
fluorescent tubes

Support for glass

Single Bulb
48" Fluorescent
Fixture

Folding
table legs

Light table, side view

table box to receive the glass that will be set into it. A router will do this job neatly and quickly.

3. To make the box more reflective and brighter, paint it white inside and out, using a good quality alkyd semi-gloss paint.

4. Install two four-foot single bulb fluorescent fixtures onto the floor of the light table box. If you are at all unsure about how to wire these fixtures, be safe, not sorry. Have a knowledgeable person help you with it. Choose full spectrum tubes for the fixtures. These give a better light all around and are easier on the eyes too.

5. Wire the fixtures to a standard wall switch, which you should mount onto the front side of the light table box. From the light switch you should connect the power cord that will go to the wall outlet. Don't skip the light switch. You will regret it, because without it you will constantly be plugging the cord in and out. And, be sure that the fixtures are properly grounded so that when you spill your coffee and it leaks into the light box, you will not light up like a Christmas tree.

6. Under the light table box, install a pair of folding table legs. These legs are just right for the table to end up at a comfortable working height for most people. Make sure they are screwed on securely. You will discover that the light table, equipped with these legs, is now portable.

7. Be sure to cut openings in both ends of the light table box to allow for the installation and removal of fluorescent tubes. The holes need only be large enough for your hands to reach into the box so you can turn the tubes out of their fixtures.

# BUILDING A GRINDING/BUFFING CENTER

For most novice woodcarvers, the business of setting up a grinding/buffing station is somewhat disconcerting; most publications tell you how to sharpen tools, not how to set up your carving space for sharpening.

There are a lot of hi-tech solutions out there for getting your tools razor sharp. But hi-tech usually translates into high-cost. With a little know-how, you can produce tools that are razor sharp without the hi-tech cost. This section discusses how to build your own low cost, safe and effective grinding/buffing station for your carving studio.

# The grinding station

A safe and effective grinder can be built from spare parts at a low cost.

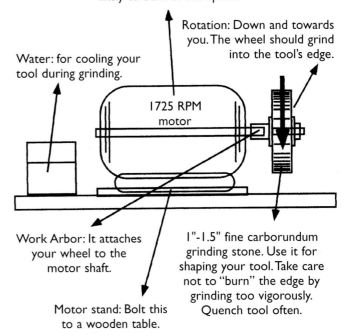

Motor should not be any faster. Tools edges are less likely to burn at this speed.

Rotation: Down and towards you. The wheel should grind into the tool's edge.

Water: for cooling your tool during grinding.

1725 RPM motor

Work Arbor: It attaches your wheel to the motor shaft.

1"-1.5" fine carborundum grinding stone. Use it for shaping your tool. Take care not to "burn" the edge by grinding too vigorously. Quench tool often.

Motor stand: Bolt this to a wooden table.

Grinding Station

For your grinding station, start by finding an old washing machine motor that rotates at 1725 rpm, and is mounted to a stand with rubber insulators. Older washing machine motors, the ones that have good strong cases and oil caps, are the ones to look for. The 1725 rpm requirement is also important. Most store-bought shop grinders (the two-wheel type) run at 3500 rpm, a speed at which it is very easy to burn or break tools. At 1725 rpm, the margin of safety increases by a factor of four, and you are much less likely to burn the tool during the grinding process.

Next, buy a work arbor and fasten it to the shaft of the motor. Work arbors come in 1/2" and 5/8" sizes and can be purchased at most hardware stores. Attach your grinding wheel to the work arbor. The grinding wheel can be an all-purpose carborundum wheel with a fine grit, commonly found at hardware stores for under $10. You can also get a "white" grinding wheel (aluminum oxide with a soft bond and open structure) that grinds at lower temperatures. Although these white wheels are nice to use, they cost more than the standard gray all-purpose.

Make sure the wheel rotates down and toward you, as indicated in the diagram. This is not so much a safety concern as proper grinding technique. The wheel should always cut into the tool edge, not off the tool edge. This way the wheel removes metal cleanly from the tool's edge instead of depositing a large burr at the edge of the tool.

Finally, take some safety precautions. Keep a little water close by to cool the tool you are sharpening from time to time. Wear safety glasses. Build a switch into your workbench that will allow you to switch the motor on and off easily. I use a simple light switch mounted into a metal receptacle box. For a nice finishing touch, add a tool-rest and a stone-guard.

# The buffing station

You can also build your own low-cost buffing station.

To assemble a buffing station, you'll need to get another electric motor, this time one with a shaft sticking out both ends. Get two work arbors and fasten them to the shafts. One arbor has to have standard thread; the other an opposite thread, so the nuts do not loosen as a result of rotation. The buffing station pictured here makes use of a mandrel, pulley and V-belt.

One of the buffing wheels needs to be made of hard felt, about 1 1/2" X 6", which you can purchase at any lapidary shop (a rock shop where they work with stones), jewelry supply store or your local carving supply store.

The second wheel needs to be a stitched cloth wheel, about 1" x 6". These are easier to find at your local hardware store, but be careful of the quality of the wheel. It should not be too flexible. The more stitching it has, the stiffer it will be—and that is what you should look for.

Position the motor so the wheels rotate up and away from you. Buffing cannot be done without the wheel rotating off the end of the tool. The hard felt wheel allows you to buff a tool quickly, without rounding the edge, and even allows you to shape a tool to a small degree. The stitched cloth wheel allows you to put an even finer edge on the tool, and to clean it up a bit before you put it into the wood.

As far as polishing compounds go, look for green compound (Tripoli) or a "stainless" compound. These are general-use compounds that work well in a great variety of buffing situations.

Load the compound on the buffing wheels by starting the motor and then shutting off the switch. While the motor is spinning down, apply the buffing compound stick to the wheel. This allows more of the compound to end up on the wheel, rather than on the wall behind the wheel. Repeat the on-off sequence a few times until the wheels are loaded. Subsequent use and repeated application of compound to the wheel will eventually load the wheel to the point where it is fully charged with compound.

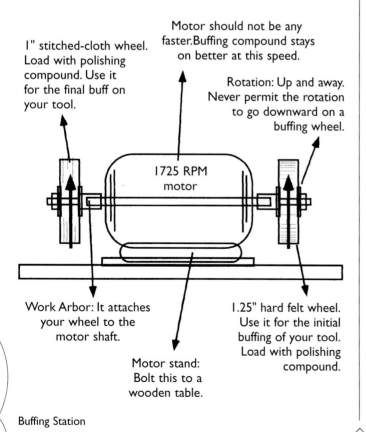

1" stitched-cloth wheel. Load with polishing compound. Use it for the final buff on your tool.

Motor should not be any faster. Buffing compound stays on better at this speed.

Rotation: Up and away. Never permit the rotation to go downward on a buffing wheel.

1725 RPM motor

Work Arbor: It attaches your wheel to the motor shaft.

Motor stand: Bolt this to a wooden table.

1.25" hard felt wheel. Use it for the initial buffing of your tool. Load with polishing compound.

Buffing Station

## The rest of the story

Even with all this sharpening hardware in place—motors, grinding wheels, bench stone, slip stones and compounds—there is still one thing that is missing. It's experience. A tool can be sharp and polished, but fail to perform properly when in the wood. Cutting angles, fulcrum-ridges, micro-bevels and a dozen other considerations can affect the way your tools work in the wood. Experience never comes cheap, but with persistence, it does come.

# CONSTRUCTING A RELIEF CARVING BENCH

## Stand-alone bench plans

Relief carvers do not often have the luxury of carving

The best way to get the perfect workbench is to make one yourself.

in the living room in front of the TV. For the most part, they need a solid workbench on which to work and place their many tools. I know from experience that many of the workbenches used by carvers are of the small, wiggly, light-weight, low-to-the-ground variety and are poorly equipped for holding a relief panel securely.

When I started carving many years ago, I used a wall-mounted workbench in my landlord's garage. It was narrow, saturated with motor oil and soiled with iron filings. This was not a good place to carve. But it was all I had.

Later, I moved up to a Black and Decker Workmate™ which was at least clean and had sturdy plastic benchdogs mounted into a moveable top. The problem was that I had to either bend over to carve, or I had to sit on a chair. Both these positions were very awkward and uncomfortable. Add to this the fact that the Workmate liked to travel across the floor when I used the mallet on my tools, and you can see why I don't use the Workmate for carving today.

My next workbench was found at an auction. It was a full-sized carpenter's workbench, made of beech wood, with two rows for square bench-dogs, an end vise and a side vise. After it was repaired, it served me for years as the place where I did all my carving. It was a real treasure.

However, it was also too low. Being a mere 32" high, it forced me to lean over my work all the time. Eventually I built some lifts for the bench legs to raise the table another 6". That helped a lot. Still, things were not as they should be. The bench-dogs were square, of the type carpenters like, and the bench top had a tool tray along the length of the top which reduced the size of the carving area. Maybe I was just too fussy for my own good. Then again, maybe I just realized that if I was going to continue to spend fifteen or twenty hours each week carving, I might as well be comfortable and well equipped.

The bench described below is one that I built about three years ago to better equip my shop for carving classes. It has proven sturdy, comfortable, durable and convenient. Some of my students have copied the design and built their own. Perhaps it can serve you as well as it has served me.

## Overview of the bench

Looking at the side view, you can see that the bench is over 39" tall. This height is good for people of average height, from 5' 9" to 6' 2". If you are taller or shorter, you will need to adjust the length of the end posts to suit your height. When working at the proper height, you will be able to lean into the table with your hip and place your arm and elbow on the table top comfortably as you carve. The foot rest, which adds stability to the table, also allows you to lift one leg while you work, taking the strain off your lower back.

Note that the table is almost 50" long. This is large enough that you can spread your tools on the bench top while you work and still have lots of room for your carving panel. This also allows for efficient use of wood if you are purchasing rough lumber in eight-foot lengths. Usually rough lumber is a bit longer than eight feet. The boards (excluding the end-caps) that make up the bench top need to be 44 1/2" long. You will have room in each 8' board to cut two lengths of boards for your bench top.

The vise is your typical 7" Record™ vise with a 9" opening capacity. It is inexpensive and relatively easy to mount under your workbench. The vise I purchased came with excellent mounting instructions. These vises come with a single dog which, when coupled with your bench dogs, will allow you to hold your carving panels at three points. This is the preferred method of holding a relief panel on a bench top.

A typical 7" Record-type vise with a 9" opening will suit most of your relief carving needs.

The vise should be mounted on the side of the bench, not the end, and close to one corner of the bench. This will allow you to move around the table as you carve and to reach your relief panel from three sides. It also leaves the rest of the table clear for your tools, drawings and the like.

Look at the top view on the bench. Note how the bench-dog holes are arranged in three rows. The inside row is staggered in relation to the two outside rows. The holes are 4" o.c. apart length-wise, but about 6" o.c. apart width-wise. This arrangement allows you to hold your carving panel with two or three points of contact, including, of course, the vise-dog.

## Tools that you will need:

1. Table saw or radial arm saw: to cut boards to length and to make the open mortise-and-tenon joints.
2. Jointer: to flatten boards prior to planing, and for dressing the edges of the boards prior to gluing.
3. Planer: to surface the boards to the correct thickness.
4. Bandsaw: to rip boards to lengthwise, and to cut the crescent under the bottom horizontal member of the end post assembly.
5. A sander: to smooth the bench components prior to fin-

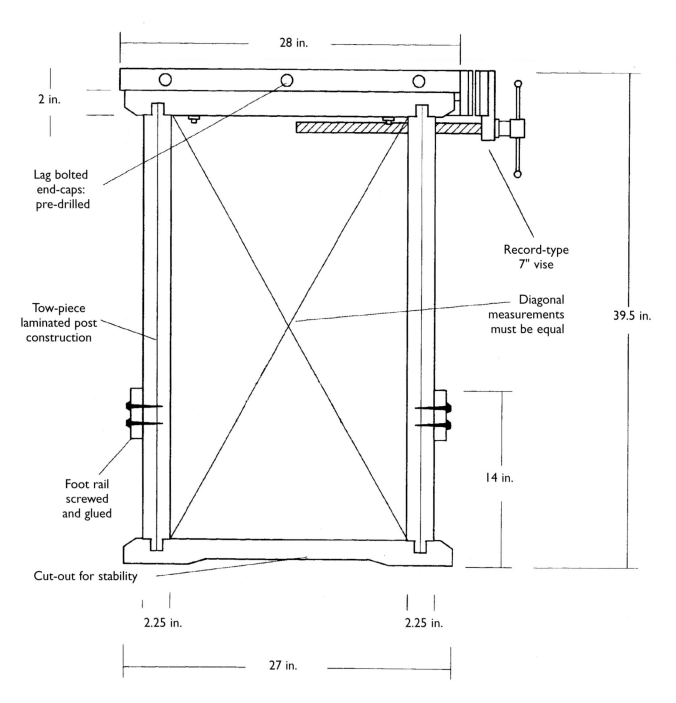

28 in.

2 in.

Lag bolted
end-caps:
pre-drilled

Record-type
7" vise

Tow-piece
laminated post
construction

Diagonal
measurements
must be equal

39.5 in.

Foot rail
screwed
and glued

14 in.

Cut-out for stability

2.25 in.

2.25 in.

27 in.

Relief Carver's Bench, end view

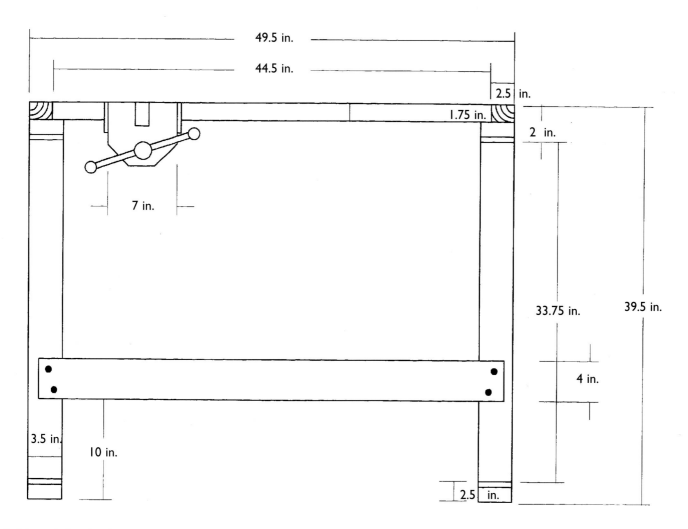

Relief Carver's Bench, side view

ishing. Palm sanders work well; belt sanders are too aggressive and leave coarse scratches on the surface.
6. Glue: use a good yellow carpenters glue. Be sure to keep your shop well above 60°C when gluing your boards.
7. Various C-clamps to help align the boards, and at least five bar clamps.
8. Paint brush and a can of quick-dry urethane finish.
9. Various bolts and screws, along with a $3/8$" drill and spurred spade bits.
10. Lots of strong coffee.

# Building the bench

### Constructing the bench top:

Start by choosing wood. I have made benches of beech, hickory, maple, oak, ash and birch. All of these woods work well, but my favorite is hickory. This is one tough wood, and though it is a little harder to work with, its weight and durability are its outstanding attributes. Hickory looks nice and is less expensive than many other woods.

Do not use softwoods like pine, cedar or even fir to make your table. And stay away from the softer hardwoods

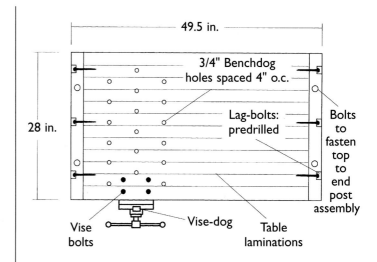

Relief Carver's Bench, top view

like basswood, alder and aspen. These woods will not stand up to the wear and tear that relief carving inflicts on a workbench. Bench dogs crush these woods easily as pressure is applied by the vise, and soon the dog holes will widen and become too sloppy to use.

Choose boards that are a full eight-feet-plus long, and as close to 2" thick as possible. Boards that are 6", 8" or even 10" wide are quite acceptable. Make sure the lumber is dry and reasonably straight. Lumber that is not fully seasoned will shrink and warp after the table is assembled, bringing you disappointment and grief. Crooked lumber is just plain hard to work with in 4' lengths.

Cut the boards to length plus one-half inch. After they are assembled in a panel, you can trim them to the finished length. Also take time to rip the boards length-wise into smaller widths. A 6" wide board should be ripped to 3", an 8" board to 4" and a 10" board to 5". That way they will fit onto a standard 6" jointer for the initial surfacing.

You will need to surface the boards (face down, not edge down) initially on a jointer to get one flat surface. Then put your boards through a planer to give the boards parallel sides and a consistent thickness. Be sure to take off only as little wood as necessary while planing. You want your bench top to be as thick as the wood allows.

Once you have boards that are flat and parallel on both faces you are ready to joint their edges in preparation for lamination. Edges should be jointed at exactly 90°. If you have any doubt as to the proper techniques for jointing wood, please take the time to consult with a cabinet maker. There are a few tricks that will help you get accurate joints and nearly flawless laminations.

Once the boards are jointed, separate them according to width so that you can make two roughly equal panels. You will need to glue the boards into two panels, so that you can put them through a planer before joining them together to form the bench top. Most small shop planers are around 14"-16" in width.

After the boards are laminated into separate panels, plane each of these panels to smooth their surfaces. Then joint the two edges that are to be glued and laminate the two smaller panels to form a complete bench top. When the glue has set, hand plane the seam connecting the two panels to make sure it is relatively smooth. Cut the bench top panel to length, taking great care to ensure that the finished panel is dimensionally accurate and square (measure the diagonals).

Fabricate end-caps so they will fit closely to the ends of the bench top panel. Then, with all your clamps in place, glue the end-caps to the panel. This is a tricky procedure that will likely require are extra pair of hands and a bit of adjustment of the two pieces if you are to get a good fit. You may also have to use glue with gap filling properties, or mix your glue with a small amount of fine sawdust. While the glue is setting in the clamps, pre-drill three countersunk holes to receive the lag bolts that will help secure the end caps to the bench top panel. Install the lag bolts using a ratchet and socket. Finally, chamfer the edges of the bench top and sand the surface.

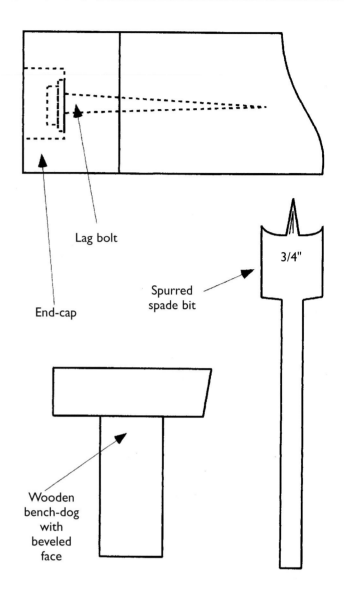

Lag bolt

End-cap

Spurred spade bit

3/4"

Wooden bench-dog with beveled face

Relief Carver's Bench, side bar

### Building the end post assemblies:

The joint used to attach the posts to the upper and lower horizontal pieces is a simple open mortise-and-tenon joint. You can make this joint using only a radial arm saw or a table saw if you need to. The joint does not have to be perfect. But make sure the joint is a snug fit, and use lots of glue with some sawdust mixed in for good measure.

Use clamps to hold the end post assemblies together while the glue sets. Take special care to ensure that the end posts are square (measure the diagonals) as you tighten the clamps. If these assemblies glue up crooked, you may as well throw the end posts out and start over again. Here, close is not good enough. Your bench will never stand evenly unless the end posts are square.

The posts are made of two pieces of wood laminated together (for stability and to achieve a larger dimension) and machined to size. This is necessary because the posts are 2$^1/_2$" thick and 3$^1/_2$" wide. I find that a thick post will transfer the impact of your mallet blows to the floor more effectively than a skinny post.

Use your band saw to cut a wide crescent from the bottom horizontal member of the end post assembly as shown in the End View, page 26. This will help the bench remain steady on a floor that is a little uneven.

### Attach bench top to end post assemblies:

You will need two machine bolts on each end of the bench top to fasten it to the end post assemblies (see Bench Top View, page 27). The bolts should be pre-drilled and countersunk (see Side Bar View, page 28) below the surface of the bench top. I used $^3/_8$" bolts with washers top and bottom. Use a spade bit to drill the holes.

Do not glue the bench top to the end post assemblies, otherwise you will be unable to remove the bench top in the event you wish to transport the table. You may also need to alter or adapt the bench top in order to customize it for your special needs at some later date. With a removable bench top, this will be a lot easier.

### Attach foot rails:

The foot rails should be constructed of 1" material to the dimensions shown in the diagrams. Chamfer the edges of the prepared boards. Fasten them to the table (be sure they are level) with glue and screws. Omit the glue if you wish to be able to fully disassemble your bench for transport or storage.

Purchase a 7" Record-type vise and install it onto the underside of the bench top near the left corner of one side. If you are left handed, you might want to do it the opposite way (see Bench Top View, page 27). Use round-headed machine bolts to fasten the vise, and be sure to pre-drill and countersink the holes that the bolts pass through. You may have to shim the vise under the table so that it does not stick up above the top surface of the bench top. Use plywood for your shim material.

### Attach Vise:

You can make some hardwood jaw plates and screw them onto each inside face of the vise. That way you will be less likely to mar your projects when you clamp them in the vise.

### Drill bench-dog holes:

Round bench-dog holes are the best and the easiest holes to make and use. They can be drilled with a $^3/_4$" spurred spade bit to receive a $^3/_4$" wooden or metal bench dog. I used metal bolts (brass or steel) until a friend turned some nice maple bench dogs for me.

Stagger the hole pattern as illustrated in the Bench Top View, page 27. Take care that you position the bench-dog holes so that they do not interfere with the vise assembly below. I find that three rows of holes allow me the most flexibility for positioning my relief panels, espe-cially round or irregular panels.

The bench-dogs should have one flat face that is slightly beveled under, so that the top edge of the dog bites your relief carving a little bit. This will help the dogs grip your carving panel better, and prevent the panel from lifting off the bench top when it is being clamped in place.

### Finishing the bench:

I used a quick-dry satin urethane product to finish my bench because it wears well and does a nice job of bring-ing out the beauty of the wood. First I applied a diluted coat, let it dry overnight, and then sanded it before apply-ing the final coat.

I also took care to avoid dripping the full strength ure-thane finish into the bench-dog holes. The more finish that drips into the holes, the tighter the holes get. You will have to take a round file to open the holes until they are large enough to again receive the bench dogs.

## Variations on the theme

If you need a larger bench you can either make the

A wall-mounted workbench is another option for relief carvers.

top thicker, or you can double the thickness of the outer 4" of the perimeter of the top to strengthen it. Otherwise your bench top will have too much spring in it and will cause your tools to bounce around annoyingly. A springy bench top also absorbs mallet blows, reducing their ability to effectively drive tools through the wood.

You can raise or lower the table height without having to modify the bench in any other way. You can add a second vise if you place it near the opposite corner of the bench. And you can add a shelf across the two foot rails to hold tools, wood or whatever. The added weight of items placed on this shelf will help to steady the bench somewhat.

### The wall-mounted bench

Often times there is not enough room in your carving area for a free standing workbench, so a more compact model needs to be constructed. This version will allow for carving from the front only, and will use the wall for support on the back and two posts on the front. Likewise, the vise will be mounted to the front of the table. Bench dogs (the round variety) can be used on the bench top.

An advantage of this style of workbench is that you can easily use wall-mounted tool racks for all your tools, keeping them close at hand and stored safely out of the way. Another advantage is that with the table being securely mounted to a solid wall, it is less likely to wobble about than its free-standing counterpart. The space under this table will allow for a foot rest and some storage too.

### Tilting workbench

One of the traditional workbenches used by relief carvers is the tilting table bench. This bench has a top that can be raised to a comfortable angle so that you can then carve while seeing the carving from the same angle as it will eventually be viewed hanging on the wall. It also allows you to carve sitting down on a stool. A few tilting benches allow you to rotate the table as well.

The greatest disadvantage of the tilting bench is that there is no place on it for your tools, so another table needs to be close by. But there is another disadvantage, too. A flat bench allows the carver to put his body behind the tool when carving, both for added power and greater control. A sitting carver cannot lean into his tools in the same way.

Carving in the softer hardwoods like butternut and basswood works better on a tilting table than carving in the harder hardwoods like birch, maple and oak. The softer woods do not require heavy strokes or the added weight of the body behind them.

When your bench is finished, carve a little design or your name into it. That will personalize your bench nicely.

# 3 WOODS FOR RELIEF CARVING

## CHOOSING THE RIGHT WOOD

Seasoned wood, as opposed to kiln-dried wood, is better for relief carvings.

A relief panel, like anything fashioned out of wood, needs to be constructed from seasoned wood. I think the term "seasoned" comes from the fact that lumber always takes several seasons to air-dry to the point where it is stable and dry enough to be used in furniture, carvings, construction and the like. Ignoring for the moment that some lumber producers kiln-dry their wood, which speeds up the drying process dramatically, hardwoods require one year per inch of thickness to properly air dry. That makes four seasons per inch of thickness; two years or eight seasons for lumber that is two inches thick.

Kiln-dried wood does not take even one season to dry but the resulting wood is not as high in quality as sea-

soned wood. The kiln-drying process places huge stresses upon the lumber and causes many side-effects, such as internal checking and case-hardening. Internal checks are cavities within the board that are not always visible from the end or the outside of the board. Case-hardening is the amount of compression the "shell" (the outside surfaces of the board) is under due to the rapid shrinking of the outside of the board. The more compression on the shell, the more twisting, cupping and warping the lumber will exhibit as it is machined and carved. If at all possible, avoid kiln-dried wood for your relief panels.

### Buy rough lumber rather than planed lumber

Most planed wood you find in lumber stores is reduced to a 1 1/2" thickness; rough lumber is close to a full 2" thick. If I use rough lumber, I can end up with a panel that is 1 3/4" thick at the end of the milling process for laminating a panel. This extra thickness allows more wood in which to render a pattern.

### Hardwoods or softwoods?

Hardwoods are almost always preferred over softwoods for relief carving. Hardwoods are from deciduous trees (leafy trees that drop their leaves seasonally). Softwoods come from trees that are evergreen and resinous. Oak, maple, birch, ash, cherry, basswood, butternut, walnut and mahogany are all hardwoods. Pine, redwood, spruce and fir are examples of softwood species.

The resins in some softwood species present problems for relief carvers. They are messy to work with and tend to "bleed" even after the carving is finished. However, it is mostly the grain structure of softwood species that makes softwoods unsuitable for relief carving.

Softwoods have growth rings that consist of a thick, soft layer sandwiched between thin tough membranes. The thin membranes require a lot more pressure from the tool-edge before they "give way" than do the soft layers sandwiched between. As the tool-edge presses on the tough membrane, the soft under-layer compresses and rips apart, leaving a distinct, rough cut behind. Even the sharpest hand tool cannot cut these woods cleanly.

Cedars are especially poor for carving with hand tools, but redwoods and pine are not far behind. Any carving done in these woods will require a lot of sanding afterward and the use of sealer/filler finishes to fill the voids left by ripped wood.

### Dangerous woods (fungus, mold, spalting, poisons)

I was once working with a wood called African walnut (otherwise known as Mansonia and not a true walnut) and could not understand why my eyes were watering as I sawed the lumber, or why I started sneezing and wheezing as never before. It turns out that this species contains many ingredients that are extremely toxic and can produce reactions like I was experiencing.

However, there are woods that are nearly as dangerous over the long run without producing symptoms as dramatic as these. Wood dust, especially from lumber that is spalted (discolored by fungus during the seasoning process) can cause long term problems with your lungs. So can the many cedars that are used in furniture, molding and mask carving. Some people are sensitive to the chemicals in birch, especially yellow birch. It is wise to investigate the woods you intend to use for issues of safety and to take precautions to reduce the amount of dust that you inhale.

## What to look for in a hardwood board

After deciding on the species of wood you wish to use, knots are the next consideration when selecting a board at the lumber yard. Most boards, except the very select (and expensive) boards, have a knot or two in them. You will want to avoid big knots and knots that will cause you to waste wood due to their location. Sometimes small knots are superficial and can be carved out or at least placed so that they will be outside the boundary of the pattern after it is transferred to the panel.

Knots are always surrounded by an area of grain that rises or falls dramatically. This makes for difficult carving, as you will have to constantly change direction as you carve in order avoid ripping the wood.

Color is another consideration. Avoid lumber that has a lot of heartwood, especially if the heartwood is much darker than the sapwood. The sapwood side of the board is most often the side that you will carve. For example, if the heartwood in a 2"-thick panel extends closer than one inch to the carved side, choose another board. Dramatic changes in color compete with the carved relief for attention and visibility. It looks horrible when an otherwise splendid figure, say a portrait of a friend, has a dark streak of heartwood crossing it. Heartwood is also usually flawed with checks and softer wood, making it less suitable than the firmer sapwood for carving.

Warp and twist are other faults to avoid in a board. Warp (cupping along the length of a board) is less difficult to deal with than twist (a long spiral). When you cut your board into small lengths for laminating into a panel, most of the warp is eliminated, and what is left will disappear quickly during the milling process. But twist is harder to eliminate and consumes more of the board's thickness during milling. Keep in mind that few boards are without either warp or twist. It is a matter of degree.

End-checks are the tiny splits visible at the end of a board, caused by shrinkage during the drying process.

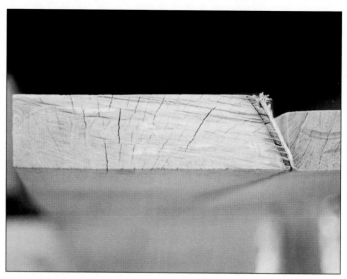
Wood with end checks, tiny splits on the end of a board, will need to be removed.

End-checking can be reduced, even eliminated, by sealing the ends of green lumber with paint or wax before storing them. However, most lumber, especially the air-dried variety will have some end-checking. If it is severe, you will waste several inches on each end of the board trying to eliminate it.

Face-checking occurs as the wood shrinks during the drying process. Kiln-dried wood is more likely to have these flaws, which appear as thin lengthwise splits on the face of the board. This is because kiln drying is stressful to lumber, causing it to shrink too rapidly, and results in splits. Air-dried lumber will have far less checking. Like knots, face-checks must be cut out of the wood or filled with glue.

Spalting is the discoloration of wood due to the growth of bacteria on the surface. If green lumber is not properly separated when stacked for drying, moisture will remain on the surface between boards, inviting bacteria to grow into colonies. Bacteria stains the wood, sometimes right through the thickness. Although wood turners love the color of spalted wood, the discoloration is less than attractive in relief carvings because it competes with the

Discoloration on a board is often due to spalting, the stain left behind by bacteria growing on the wood.

relief for visibility. Besides this, spalted wood is not healthy to work.

Sometimes lumber contains "punky" areas, that is areas that are soft and spongy, having partially decomposed in the log before being cut into lumber. Punky wood is good for nothing and must be removed before laminating.

Wane is the "bark edge" of the board. It must be cut out of the lumber before lamination can begin, unless, of course, you wish to incorporate the wane in the design of the carving.

Relief carvers delight in finding boards with straight grain that rises gently in one direction. It allows them to

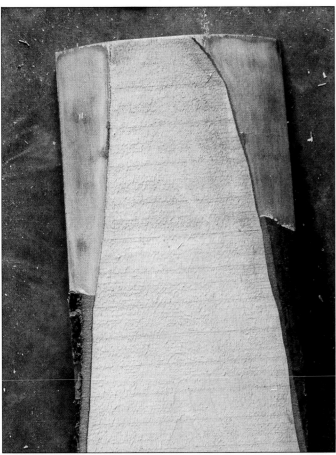

The bark edge of the board, or wane, will need to be removed unless you plan to incorporate it into the design.

carve the wood easily without having to constantly change the direction of their tools. Look at the edge of a rough board and observe the rise of the grain along the length of the board. If the rise is gentle and predictable, then go ahead and buy that board. But if the grain rises and falls repeatedly along the length it will make for more work to carve the wood cleanly. However, if you desire a lively surface grain pattern in the carving, the extra work demanded by a changeable grain will be worth the effort.

Color is important too. Choose wood that is light in color if you want your finished carving to look bright and stand out in low-light conditions like those found in the average home. Dark woods hide much of the relief you

spend so much time carving. I prefer woods with colors that are warm and contain a brown hue or "cast:" red oak is red-brown; white birch is butter-brown; maple is silver-brown; and yellow birch is liquid-honey brown. Woods with other colors are useful too. Tulipwood has a green cast, as does black locust. Damanu, an exotic wood, has a wine-brown cast, and some Mahoganies are quite red, almost like burgundy when clear-finished. These four examples will look out of place in most homes unless allowances are made for them in the color scheme.

## The difference between figure and grain

Grain has to do with the direction of wood fibers and the layering of growth rings along the length of a board. Terms like "carving with the grain" and "carving against the grain" are used to explain the best approach to carve a piece of wood considering the direction of the wood fibers and layers of the growth rings.

Figure is the interplay of grain pattern and color on the surface of the board. Highly figured boards have a lively grain pattern, lots of reflectivity and variation in color. Zebra wood is an example of a highly figured wood. So are elm and mahogany. Basswood, on the other hand, has almost no figure at all. It is important to choose wood with a subdued figure so that the figure does not compete with the relief for visibility.

## Preferred woods for relief carving

**Birch** (northern white): This is my favorite relief carving wood. It is locally available and fairly inexpensive, but it also has many admirable qualities. It machines and glues very well. It takes stains reliably. It carves easily, leaving a polished cut, and holds fine detail. Its grain structure is close, and its figure (noticeable grain pattern) is subdued. It is a bright, reflective and lively wood that responds well to changes in light and shows well in low-light situations. It sometimes shows dramatic variations in color between the usually butter-colored sapwood and the orange-brown or brown/purple heartwood.

**Birch** (yellow, eastern): This wood is similar to northern white birch, except that is a liquid-honey color, denser and harder to carve. However, even the best samples are not as reflective or lively as those found in white birch.

**Maple** (hard): Although much harder than birch, maple is a delightful wood to carve and my second preference. It has many of the reflective properties of white birch, holds the tiniest detail, and machines, glues and stains well. Its color is silver-brown. Unless you love a challenge, stay away from varieties of maple like "birds-eye" and "ribbon."

**Maple** (soft): This wood is similar in appearance to hard maple, but not nearly as dense. Neither does it carve as cleanly. But it holds detail well enough if your tools are sharp and will produce attractive carvings. One species of soft maple is Mississippi silver maple.

**Red Oak:** This wood has many delightful characteristics including a soft red-brown color and a bold grain and figure. The grain structure makes it somewhat of a challenge to carve as there are tough, thick membranes sandwiching porous layers. But it carves well as long as you do not expect it to hold fine detail. You need to design your carving so that the coarse grain of the oak enhances, rather than competes with, the design. The rule of thumb is keep it simple and bold.

**White Oak:** Similar to red oak, but quite a bit harder, white oak has more color variation, which can compete with the relief for visibility.

**Ash:** This wood is much like red oak, but has a blonde color overall. It holds moderately fine detail.

**Elm:** This wood carves well and is stable, but it has a very busy figure more suited for wood turnings and furniture than relief.

**Hickory:** Here is a hard wood, indeed! Yet, if you manage to prepare a panel for carving so that the dark heartwood does not intrude into the area being carved, the wood carves well and looks lovely. In a 2"-thick panel, I always place the heartwood to the back and make sure that there is at least 1" of sapwood above it. The sapwood is a sun-bleached blonde color. The grain is not quite as coarse as red oak and has no porous layers. It holds moderately fine detail.

**Beech:** Beech is a beautiful, but hard wood. It carves very well and hold great detail. It might be a little hard to find samples that are consistent in color.

**Cherry:** Cherry is also a fine relief carving wood, though it tends to rip slightly when carving end-grain. Color variations within a single board can be a little troublesome too. Make sure the sample you select has consistent color and not too many mineral steaks in it. It holds moderately fine detail.

**Alder:** This is a light wood with an unusual figure, but with a lovely warm brown-sugar color to it. It does not carve as well a some of the others, ripping frequently when cutting the end-grain, but it is a light wood, fairly soft and reasonably priced. It holds moderate detail.

**Mahogany** (Honduras): This is a relatively soft carving wood which holds moderate detail, laminates well, is quite stable and has a warm color. But it can be expensive, and sometimes the color is too dark for relief carvings that will be displayed indoors. The grain in this species can be a challenge at times, with the rise of the grain alternating every inch or so in some samples. This wood has good reflective properties and is especially suited for sign making.

**Teak:** This wood is durable and holds moderate detail. But it is an oily wood, filled with fine, abrasive sand. It can dull your tools quickly. Add to this the fact that teak does not accept finishes easily (because of the oil in it) and resists glue unless the jointed edges are first wiped clean of oil with a cloth dipped in mineral spirits. Teak is also a little dark and will appear dull unless finished with many coats of quality teak oil. All in all, this is a wood you should use only if there is a specific need for it.

**Basswood:** This is one of the most common relief carving woods used today. But it is, in my humble opinion, also the dullest, most boring wood for relief carving. It is a stringy wood that leaves "fuzzies" behind. It almost always looks better if stained, but staining is a somewhat tricky process because of the variation in absorbency in the wood. (Try sealing it first before finishing with stain.) Basswood carves easily and holds moderate detail. It also laminates well, but is only moderately stable, tending to cup to the carved side more than other hardwoods. It has a close grain with almost no figure (noticeable grain pattern).

**Tuliptree** (Yellow Poplar): This wood is similar to basswood, except that it has a greenish cast. It is stringy, fuzzy and rather dull in appearance. It carves easily and holds moderate detail.

**Butternut:** This is another widely used wood, primarily because it is soft and can mostly be carved without a mallet. However, this wood also lacks character, and has a busy figure that competes with the relief for visibility. Butternut holds moderate detail. It is darker than many other relief carving woods, making it less suitable for carvings that will be displayed in low-light situations. This species is rapidly diminishing in availability due to a widespread fungus disease.

**Walnut:** Walnut is a wonderful sculpting and furniture wood with rich color and beautiful figure. It is easy to machine, laminates and finishes well. It is also soft enough to be carved without the use of a mallet. However, it is too dark for relief carving. Its fibers are long and tend to split easily, making carving difficult at times. It is also an expensive wood. My suggestion is to leave this species to the sculptors and cabinet makers.

**Rosewood:** This species comes in many variations, all of which are expensive and increasingly hard to obtain. Without going into details, this wood is usually too dark and too highly figured to be useful for most relief carving projects.

# CONSTRUCTING A RELIEF PANEL

## PREPARING THE BOARDS
### Overview

For preparing a relief panel, you will need more than just basic hand tools. You will need a skill saw or radial arm saw to cut the boards to length, a table saw or band saw to rip the boards to width, a jointer to flatten the faces and edges of each board, glue, bar/pipe clamps of sufficient length and two C-clamps for each joint in the panel.

In my shop I use a radial arm saw to cut the boards to length. This tool is safer and more accurate than a hand-held skill saw. I use a 14" band saw to rip the boards to width. Band saws cut easily because they have a thin blade and kick back is not an issue.

My jointer is an older 6" Craftsman, with a protractor located at the fence adjuster end. I've found larger jointers are too expensive and smaller jointers are ineffective. To get the jointer to produce accurate edges, I spend some time each year leveling the in-feed table and making sure the cutter head and blades are positioned accurately. The effort is worth it, because my jointer can produce panel after panel of flawless joints with no gaps. In fact, when the carving is completed, it is hard to tell where the joints were in the original panel. Only the change in color or grain between boards gives the joint away.

My planer is a 16" Taiwanese copy of the 15" Rockwell/Delta thickness planer. It is wide enough and powerful enough to handle full-width planing, even in hard maple. I use no dowels or biscuits between the boards. these are unnecessary.

### Arranging boards

When arranging boards for laminating, I first place all the sapwood so it will be end up on the carved side of the panel. Then I arrange the grain of each board so that it rises from the bottom to the top of the panel. To do this, I look at the side of each board and choose one grain line, following along the length of the board to see which direction the grain is rising. Be especially careful at the joints between boards, so that the grain rises in the same direc-

Find the rise of the grain by choosing one grain line and following it along the length of the board.

tion between adjoining boards. Neglecting to do this will make for difficult carving across the laminations.

As a rule I also try to arrange the boards so they are vertical rather than horizontal in the finished carving. This is because vertical boards look livelier and are more reflective when light crosses them from the side, as usually happens when they are hung on a wall. If you must arrange your boards horizontally, plan to light the carving from above so that the beauty of the wood is not lost.

### Measuring and cutting the pieces

If my pattern calls for a finished size of 14" by 21", I cut my boards so that they will produce a panel 1" larger all around. For this example, I would cut the boards 22" long and make sure there is enough combined width between the boards to end up with at least 15" of width in the panel. This will allow enough room for proper placement of the pattern on the wood panel. It also gives the extra size needed in case there are last minute changes in the pattern or slight defects in the wood that can be avoided by shifting the pattern. Better to have a panel slightly larger than slightly undersize. When the pattern is completely traced onto the rough panel, it can be cut to shape on the band-saw.

Unless you add camber to your relief panel, it will look like this when you are finished carving. This is because all relief carvings cup to the carved side.

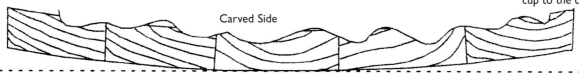

Carved Side

Back Side

## Stabilizing the panel

If you are like most relief carvers, you have experienced the problem of having your relief carving warp and cup to the carved side so that what was supposed to be a beautiful piece of craftsmanship instead became a cause for disappointment. In my early years as a carver, I faced this problem many times. Back then there were few books or clubs for carvers, let alone for relief carvers, so no matter how hard I looked I could not find a solution to this problem. The solution I present to you here is time tested, reasonable and straight forward. I hope it helps you construct relief panels that will be dimensionally stable, attractive and worthy of the work you put into them.

As all carvers know, wood swells, shrinks, twists and checks in response to temperature, humidity and machining. Even when coated with a protective finish, the wood is still likely to move a bit. However, most of us do not realize that a wood panel is most likely to twist and check when it is being carved. This is because relief carving is the process of taking away from a flat panel the very wood that helps keep it stable in the first place. Carving away a piece of wood affects all the wood that remains in the panel. Carvers preparing a panel for relief carving will have to deal with this dimensional distortion of the wood while it is being machined, but they will also have to deal with it while the panel is being carved.

Here are some preliminary things you can do to build a stable panel and for relief carving:

1. Laminate your panel as soon as you have machined the wood to size. This is important because the longer you wait, the more likely the wood will warp, cup or twist in response to changes in humidity and temperature. I never leave machined boards overnight without gluing them together into a panel. The shape and dimensional stability of a freshly machined board is temporary at best.

Furthermore, boards that are ready for lamination should be handled carefully. If you bump or drop them they will sometimes "spring" into a new shape. Neither should boards machined at a friend's shop be transported across town in cold or hot weather (relative to the temperature in the shop) for gluing into a panel. Temperature changes will cause boards to cup, warp and twist. The movement is slight, but can be enough to make a joint less than perfect.

2. Every relief panel over eight inches wide should be constructed from laminated pieces whose length equals the greatest dimension of the panel. For example, if the panel is 14" tall by 20" wide, the pieces of wood used to make the panel should be 20" long. If the panel is going to be 24" tall by 20" wide, the pieces should be 24" long. This rule applies because wood tends to cup at right angles to the length of the grain.

Laminated boards are more stable than single large

pieces of wood because the tendency of one board to cup during carving is counteracted somewhat by the piece of wood adjoining it. Think of a single board as a person with a will of his own who can go where he wants and when he wants with little to constrain him. Now think of a group of laminated boards as a committee. Everyone knows that a committee is less likely to go anywhere or do anything.

3. Use only seasoned wood. This should go without saying, but even experienced carvers occasionally use wood that they assume is dry, but which is really just a bit too moist. Carving a piece of wood exposes more surface area to drying. Wood that dries shrinks. As wood shrinks it warps. Panels that shrink more on one side than the other tend to cup. And so, as a panel is carved, it will cup to the carved side even more if it is less than properly seasoned.

4. Cut out any checks and knots in the wood. Even slight checks will turn into wide checks under the impact of mallets and chisels, and knots will be a distraction to the appearance of the finished piece.

5. Be sure that your shop is warm. If you use yellow or white glue the temperature should be about 70°F (20°C). Lower temperatures will jeopardize the ability of the molecules in the glue to "knit" together. The glue might hold for a while, but near the end of the carving process, the joints will likely fail. If you glue the boards into a panel at floor level, make sure to raise the clamped panel up to where the temperature is warmer.

Modern glues are incredibly strong and easy to use. Dowels and biscuits are not needed in the gluing process because they add no strength. Their purpose is usually to help with the alignment of the boards, however, the use of C-clamps will accomplish this with little hassle. Excess glue that seeps out from the glue joints under the pressure of the clamps can easily be removed on the carved side with a hand plane, and on the back side with a straight chisel.

## The benefits of camber

One strategy for stabilizing your relief panel that is almost unknown in the woodcarving world is adding camber—like you see in snow skis—to the panel. Years ago, I discovered that if I built some camber into my panels I could compensate for the tendency of the panel to cup to the carved side. Over the years I experimented with the amount of camber built into my panels as it relates to the cupping tendencies of various woods.

White birch, my favorite relief carving wood, tends to cup moderately, while woods like basswood and mahogany tend to cup less. But all woods cup. So far I have found no wood that is suitable for relief carving that does not cup to the carved side.

There are, of course, other precautionary measures to take. Some carvers advise that you should carve an equal

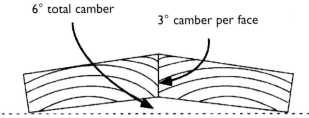

6° total camber     3° camber per face

The WRONG way to apply camber to a panel. Here the change in angle (exaggerated for clarity) is too severe.

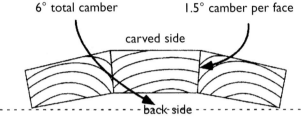

6° total camber     1.5° camber per face

carved side

back side

The RIGHT way to apply camber to a panel. Here the change in angle (exaggerated for clarity) is gradual..

amount of wood off the back of a relief in order to stabilize it against cupping. While this may work in theory, it is difficult and risky to implement. It forces the carver to carve the carving twice. How much better it would be to spend a few moments setting up your jointer so you can add some angle to each face of each joint. Even if you have to find someone with a jointer who can help you with this, adding camber is worth the effort.

### How much camber?

A panel with fewer boards requires more angle at each joint to achieve the required camber. I like to set my jointer for between 1° and 2° of angle beyond 90°. In other words, I set the fence between 91° or 92°. For example, rather than have two boards with one joint between them utilizing a 3° angle on each side of the joint (this would result in 6° of camber), I would prefer to use three boards with two joints between them, each face of the joint having 1.5° angle built into it. This also results in 6° of camber.

### Adding camber to your relief panel

Here's how I build camber into my relief panels. I pre-

A typical board used in a panel, after jointing.

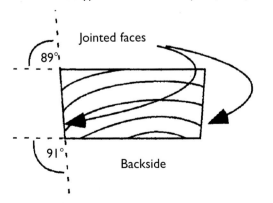

Jointed faces

89°

91°

Backside

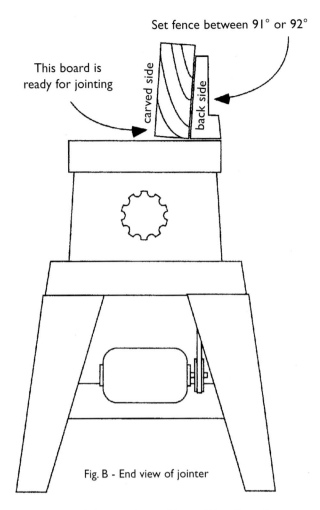

This board is ready for jointing

Set fence between 91° or 92°

carved side

back side

Fig. B - End view of jointer

pare a number of pieces of wood by cutting them to length, ripping them to widths of 3" to 4" and then planing them to thickness. I choose the surface of each board that will end up on the carved side of the panel and mark it with a pencil. Normally this is the "sapwood" side of the board, which is the clearest and lightest wood. Heartwood is placed to the back so that it does not interfere with the visibility of the relief in the finished carving.

Once I know where each board will be placed in relation to the others and which side of each board will be on the carved side of the panel, I take all the boards to the jointer. There I machine their edges in preparation for gluing. I set my jointer so that the fence is 91° or 92°. Placing the back of each board firmly against the fence, I carefully machine their edges so that they will be less than 90°. If the fence is set at 91°, then the edge of the board will end up being 89° to the carved surface of the panel and 91° to the back of the panel

If you are using four 4"-wide boards to create a 16"-wide panel, then you will have three joints in your panel. Each joint has two faces. If each face is jointed so that it is at 1° less than 90° to the carved face, each glued joint will have 2° of camber built into it. Three joints will result in 6° of camber.

Stacking the boards vertically on edge shows the slight camber added to the panel.

You have to own a jointer to do this accurately, though it is possible to use a jack plane and a jig to build camber into your panels. I used to do this manually at first, then decided that life was too short to waste time on such a finicky procedure. Shortly thereafter I purchased a used Craftsman 6" jointer.

I set the fence to 91° or 92° (depending on the amount of camber needed and the number of boards in the panel) using the protractor built into the end of the fence. The eccentrics at the clamping end of the fence make it easy to adjust. Once the fence is set to my satisfaction, I make sure each board passes over the cutters with its "carved side" facing away from the fence. In other words, you must place the back of the board against the fence. This applies the correct angle to the board's edge.

When all the boards are jointed, they can be placed on the work table. Stack them on their side in the order that they will appear in the relief panel. This way you can measure the amount of camber you have built into the panel, and also test the tightness of the joints. No gaps are

allowed. When viewed from either end, your unglued panel should present a camber of $1/8$" for a panel under 14" and perhaps $1/4$" for a panel 20" wide

If all goes well, during the carving process the panel will cup to the carved side, but only so that most but not all of the camber you built into the panel is used up. When your finished carving is hung on the wall, the remaining camber is invisible and helps the carving hang better.

## Some more tips

1. Use a record book to keep track of your attempts to build the correct amount of camber into your relief panels. Record the camber used for each species of wood you use. Such factors as the width of growth rings, moisture content of the wood, width of the finished panel and depth of the carving will play a part in your success.

2. Panels tend to cup to the carved side early on. After the majority of the wood is removed the cupping should cease. Detail work such as texturing should not affect the cupping significantly.

3. Do not use excessive clamping pressure when gluing your boards together. You may "starve" the joint of glue.

4. Use pipe clamps to clamp the boards together and use C-clamps at each joint to keep the boards from migrating out of position. After the pipe clamps have been tightened for a minute or two, the C-clamps can be removed.

5. When designing your relief panel, be aware that thick borders around your relief will increase the amount of cupping that occurs. This is why I design my relief carvings without borders or with borders that are assigned to the deepest levels of the carving.

As I mentioned, this method of stabilizing relief panels is time tested and reliable. But you must be willing to work with your wood and machinery accurately. Learn to adjust your jointer so it is able to provide you with accurate joints. Sometimes equipment falls out of adjustment because of vibration, wear or having been moved around too much. Learn to feed your boards into the jointer with even pressure and constant rate. Learn to inspect your joints for accuracy and accept no joint that is less than 100% true. The amount of work you invest in achieving accurate joints is small compared to the many hours of carving that will be invested later.

## TWO VIEWS

Laminating boards and adding camber to relief carving panels may seem like an odd practice to other woodworkers, and to cabinetmakers in particular. A cabinetmaker's rational is that wood cups to the sapwood side because of shrinkage. Because most cabinet makers do not carve into a panel, they may not realize that wood also cups due of the removal of wood during the relief carving practice.

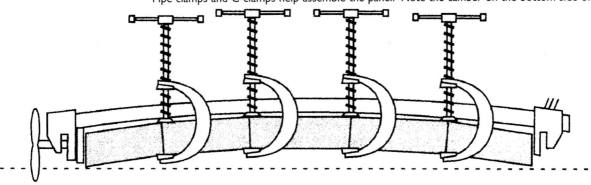

Pipe clamps and C-clamps help assemble the panel.  Note the camber on the bottom side of the panel.

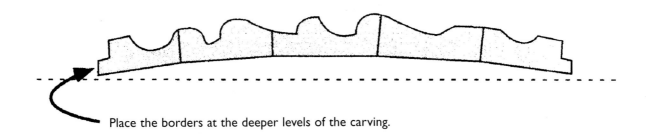

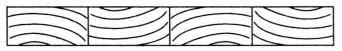

Place the borders at the deeper levels of the carving.

Because cabinetmakers are concerned only with shrinkage, cabinetmakers laminate their panels alternating the end grain of each board, so that the sapwood side of one board faces up and the sapwood of the adjoining board faces down. The idea is that the cupping of individual boards will cancel each other, leaving a laminated panel (perhaps a table top) relatively flat over all. The faces of each board are jointed to a strict 90°.

As a relief woodcarver, I do not want to orient the boards of my panels with alternating end grain. I want all the sapwood to the carved side, for the sake of color and consistency of grain. So I must find a different way to stabilize the panel. Thus the need for building camber into a relief panel.

Carpenters alternate the end grain when laminating their panels, as shown in this diagram. Relief carvers laminate their panels with all the sapwood to the carved side.

*Malamute, W.F. Judt*
*14" x 18"*
*white birch*
*Special features: Paw-print*
*border which employs the*
*"quilted" look; highly detailed fur*
*texturing all done with V-tools; com-*
*pression of depth to a 1:16 ratio.*

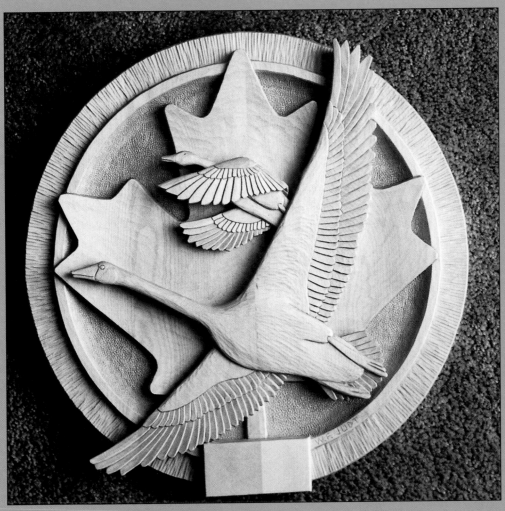

Trumpeter Swans
W.F. Judt
18" diameter
white birch
Special features: Radial tool marking on outside border; use of the techniques of relative size and overlapping to make the background bird appear farther away.

And the two shall become one, W.F. Judt
15" diameter
red oak

Give us today our daily bread, W.F. Judt
15" diameter
hard maple

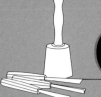

*The Lord is my light...*, W.F. Judt, 20" x 30", white birch.
Special features: Compact arrangement of the decorative text was prepared entirely on the computer.

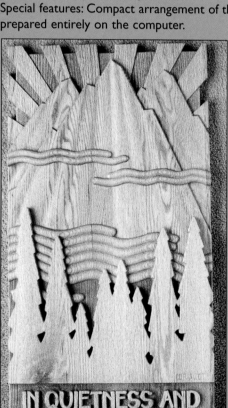

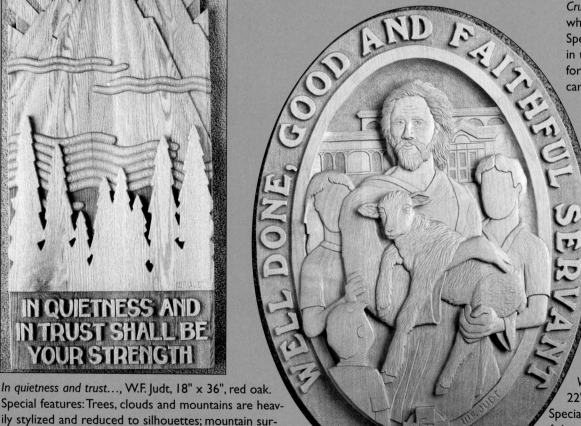

*Crucifix,* W.F. Judt, 14" x ⬜
white birch.
Special features: The gra⬜
in the arms runs horizo⬜
for strength; the figure i⬜
carved on three sides o⬜

*In quietness and trust...*, W.F. Judt, 18" x 36", red oak.
Special features: Trees, clouds and mountains are heavily stylized and reduced to silhouettes; mountain surfaces are carved like gentle waves; the rays imply the presence of God; the text is in a typeface that evokes quiet gentleness.

*Well done...*, W.F. Judt, 22" x 30", white birch.
Special features: The faces of the children are left featureless so they more easily represent all children.

*Last Supper,* W.F. Judt, 14" x 42", red oak.
Special features: Horizontal orientation of the boards that comprise the panel; use of red oak's strong figure to enhance the appearance of relief; use of hands to represent people.

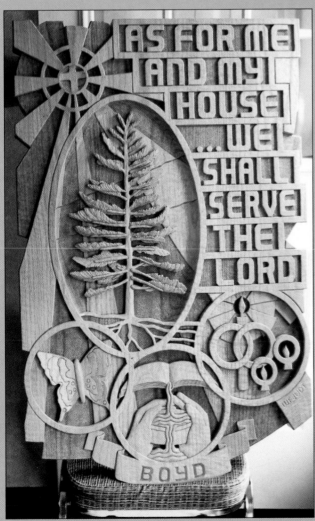

*As for me and my house,* W.F. Judt, 22" x 36", red oak.
Special features: Rays pass through and across all layers of the carving; the modular arrangement of the design components helps isolate symbols; overlapping the ellipse and the circles creates the effect of transparency.

*Marcotte Family Heirloom,* W.F. Judt, 20" x 30", red oak.
Special features: Use of maple leaves and seed pods to fill in corners; irregular perimeter adds interest to carving.

# GALLERY

*Hey, Jenny, we'll make it,* W.F. Judt, 20" x 30",
white birch.
Special features: Use of ribbon to hold text;
strategic use of seven family symbols in the
design; achieving a portrait of a family home.

*Dolphins,* W.F. Judt, 20" x 30", hard maple.
Special features: Use of relative size and overlap to
create perspective and depth; use of stamping to texture the coral reef; wave effect in the background; sea
creatures carved on border to form a repeating band;
using kelp as a design element to bring focus and
direction to the design.

*Scroll,* 14" x 18", white birch, W.F. Judt.
Special features: Scroll is carved from a single
laminated panel; incised text to create the effect
of "calligraphy;" insets carved to receive brass
plates; scrolls carved in classical style to show
forward from all four corners.

*Wild Bee Apiaries,* W.F. Judt, 22" x 25", white birch. Special features: Use of fox to introduce element of curiosity and calm to carving; use of honey combs as a repeating border; honey bees are appliqués to surface of panel.

*Jordan Lumber,* W.F. Judt, 14" x 20", cherry. Special features: Yellow pine trees accurately rendered; effective use of stamping to segregate text areas; use of layers and relative size to create depth in the landscape.

*Lion Rampant,* W.F. Judt, 12 x 12, red oak. Special features: Carved in 1975; one of my first carvings.

*Beadles Lumber,* W.F. Judt, 14" x 20", hard maple.
Special features: Accurately rendered southern white pine trees; use of silhouettes of trees in background; use of an irregular border to make the perimeter more interesting.

*Moose*, Laurette Cissell,
14" x 22", white birch.

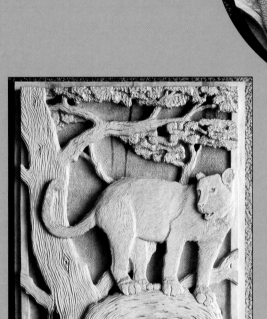

*Leopard in Tree*, Louw Smit, 14" x 16", white
birch.

*Prospector*, Ron Bush, 20" x 20", white birch.

*Abba Father*, Peter Dyck, 12" x 16", cherry.

ABBA
PAPA
DADDY
FATHER

THOSE
WHO ARE
LED BY THE
SPIRIT OF GOD
ARE SONS OF GOD

NO LONGER SLAVES
OF SIN · ROM. 6:6

*No longer slaves…*, Dennis Aicken, 18" x
18", white birch.

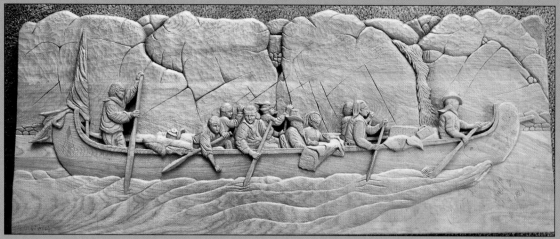

*Frontiersmen,* Hans Dietrich, 15" x 45", eastern birch.

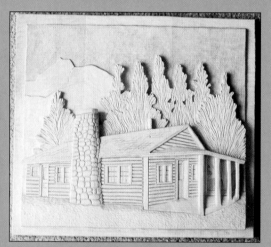

*Homestead Cabin,* Harry Quinn, 16" x 18", white birch.

*Our Puppy,* Harry Quinn, 12" x 18", eastern birch.

*One True Friend,* Sherri Réhaume, 15" diameter, hard maple.

# GALLERY

Moose in Forest, 16" x 25", white birch, Al McEwan.

Eagle Portrait, 14" diameter, yellow birch, Neil Dobson.

Book Worm, Doreen Barabash, 12" x 17", white birch.

Wild Kakwa, 16" x 24", white birch, Bob Neufeld.

## CHARACTERISTICS OF A RELIEF PATTERN

Relief patterns offer only a front view. Information about depth is marked on the pattern

A relief pattern is much different from a pattern used for sculpture or in-the-round carving. Sculpture requires a pattern with a front, side and top view, each offering a different view of an object. Relief patterns offer only the front view. There is no side view or top view. Information about depth is marked on the pattern for future reference.

Think of relief design as something akin to a stain glass window pattern, where the overall picture is made up of individual small pieces. Every piece has a shape and area, separated by lines. But whereas color adds the illusion of depth in a stained glass picture, the elements of relief and texture do this in the carving. Relief simply means the actual use of depth, compressed as it is, to add realism to a shape that is otherwise relatively flat.

In a relief pattern, objects have their own shape, borders and area and overlap each other to form layers. These layers are assigned depths relative to each other. Some parts of the pattern will be at the top level of the panel, others at $1/8$", $1/4$", $1/2$" and so on. The depth assigned to any particular object refers always to the highest point in that area. If, for instance, an object is assigned a depth of $1/4$" and the area directly below it is assigned the depth of $1/2$", then there is $1/4$" of depth in

which the higher object can be modeled and shaped.

Compression of depth is very important in relief carving design. The two dimensions of "width" and "height" are always normal, but depth is compressed anywhere from one-fifth to one-twentieth of normal. Think of the amount of relief on a common coin, where the image on the face looks normal in width and height, but when viewed from the side the depth is severely compressed. This is an extreme example of compression, but it serves to point out that the eye can be tricked to see shape and "roundness" even when depth is severely compressed.

The trick in relief is to use rounding techniques, overlap and texture to simulate normal shape on an object that is really quite compressed. It takes time to learn the tricks, but rest assured that there is not much, from portraits to landscapes, that cannot be rendered effectively in relief.

Relief carvings, unlike sculptures, are meant to be viewed from the front, hanging on a wall. Both the viewing angle and the lighting are important. If the viewer observes the relief carving from the side it will appear distorted. And if there isn't proper lighting to highlight the carving with shadows, then much of the detail, and the shape implied by this detail, will be lost to the viewer.

## DRAWING YOUR OWN PATTERNS

The main reason for drawing your own patterns is that there are very few sources for relief patterns, and even fewer patterns with unique designs. Part of the reason for the scarcity of relief patterns is that relief carvers are only now gaining some recognition for their approach to carving.

### Basic Drawing Tools

Drawing relief patterns requires just a few essentials. They include pencils, masking tape, a pantograph, a 16" clear plastic ruler, a beam compass, a regular adjustable compass, access to a photocopier, a light table, large-format (ledger size) paper, erasers, a pencil sharpener and tracing paper.

It is important to use large sheets of paper that can be joined together to form larger sheets without a lot of taped seams. I prefer ledger-size (11" x 17") sheets. Four sheets taped together (masking tape works best) allow for a relief design that is 22" x 34". Tracing paper takes pencil lines well and also erases well.

Vellum, the stuff used for blue-prints, is more expensive and less useful. It does not erase well, tends to curl, and is not transparent enough to make tracing easy or to allow you to avoid using a light table.

Carbon paper is useful for transferring the finished pattern to the wood panel, but it should not be used in the pattern-making process. It leaves a line that can not be edited or erased.

The pencils that are best suited for drawing relief patterns are labeled HB. HB pencils draw a dark line, but erase well. A softer pencil lead smudges too much and will tend to mess your pattern quickly. A harder pencil lead won't give you a dark enough line. Be sure to invest in a good pencil sharpener. You'll want to keep your pencil sharp for accurate drawing and tracing.

Erasers do not need to be exotic, just effective. I buy the white artists' erasers, which are large enough to handle easily. They are more effective than the pink or brown erasers for removing graphite lines.

Plastic rulers are invaluable in pattern drawing. They allow you to measure and draw more easily than rulers that hide the lines beneath them. I still work in standard measurements, but you may prefer metric measurements. A 16" or 20" plastic ruler is the best for drawing the longer lines used in grids, borders and design elements.

## Advanced Drawing Tools

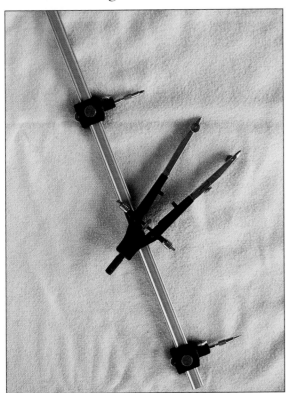

A "Y" compass and a beam compass are used to render perfect circles.

You will eventually need a compass to draw circles and divide geometric areas accurately. A regular "Y" compass is essential, but a larger "beam" compass is also required. The beam compass allows you to draw circles

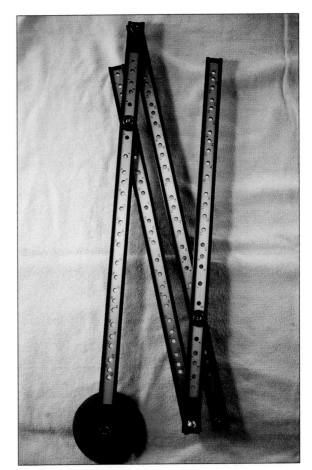

With the aid of a pantograph, you can accurately enlarge and reduce pattern elements.

from 2 inches to 6 feet in diameter. It consists of two movable attachments; one for the sharp anchor point and the other for the pencil lead. These ride an I-beam, and can be locked in place for accuracy. Most art stores carry these instruments, but you can also find them at some carving/woodworking supply stores.

A pantograph is a device for mechanical (as opposed to electronic) enlargement/reduction of a drawing. It produces an editable pencil line. When I need a design element in a particular size, the pantograph allows me to quickly scale the enlargement precisely, saving valuable time.

A light table is the final piece of drawing equipment you'll need for your work space. Commercial light tables are available, but these can be quite expensive. My light table is home-made, and I have included plans for it in this book. (See page 19.)

Photocopiers also have a place in relief carving pattern making, but only in a supporting role, not as a major player. Photocopiers allow a person to copy an image from a book, magazine, poster, greeting card or photo print so that it ends up on a piece of paper that can subsequently be placed on a light table for tracing. The photocopier is used only in the preliminary stages of design.

Photocopiers may also be used to scale a photo or

The road is directionally tool marked to lead the eye from the foreground to the background. The use of the techniques of overlap and relative size reinforce the perception of depth

drawing to a specific size, after which the scaled drawing is again brought to the light table where it is properly located and then traced onto a pattern.

On occasion, when I needed an accurate drawing of a hand, I simply placed my hand on the photocopier, in the position that I desired, and touched the "start" button. Voila! Instant image! All that I need to do is trace the photocopy image into a line drawing using my light table.

Photocopiers have limitations. One is that the lines on photocopied reproductions cannot be erased. In order to "tweak" a line, the copy has to be traced into a pencil line drawing. From there it can be refined as necessary. Scaling is also rather awkward on the photocopier. It is usually much easier to use a pantograph to do the final scaling of an object for inclusion in the pattern. Again, because the pantograph creates a pencil-line enlargement, its output is editable.

Properly used, the photocopier should provide you

with access to images that can be used as a starting point for a pattern. Unfortunately, they also present the carver with the temptation to violate copyright laws and to infringe on the rights of the artist. Make every effort to avoid blind copying. Use photocopies as a resource, not as an end in themselves.

## Drawing an Ellipse

One of the tasks I disliked early on in my carving career was trying to draw an accurate ellipse. I read up on the subject and remembered some of my geometry instruction from high school, but I was still ill-equipped to draw an ellipse to the exact dimensions that I required for a particular project.

The worst part was trying to manage the pins, paper, axes, string and pencil required to draw an accurate ellipse according to one method I call the "How to Drive Yourself Crazy" method. Even worse was the "mathematical approach," which required a person to grasp the prin-

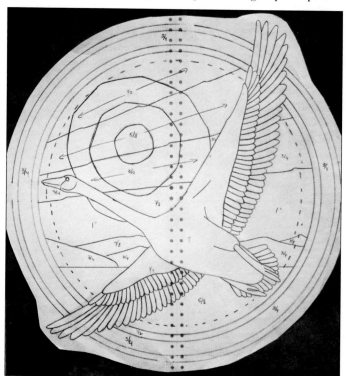

The Trumpeter swan's wings extend past the border causing the carving to appear borderless.

ciples of mathematics in order to plot out an accurate ellipse.

One evening, while teaching a class of carving students, I was trying to draw an ellipse, with the usual frustration that accompanies such a task, when a student of mine, Ron Bush (bless his heart) showed me what he termed the "trammel method." This method involves only a piece of paper, a clear plastic ruler and a pencil.

## The Trammel Method

Start with a piece of paper that will accommodate an

Honey combs reinforce the theme of this carving which has to do with bee keeping, and also provides interest along the perimeter of the carving. Trees help to fill in the corners.

In this carving titled "Kakwa Falls" the surrounding border area is the deepest layer in this carving, and serves a supporting role for the landscape on top of it. Effective use of layering reinforces depth and perspective.

*And the Two Shall Become One* shows good use of negative space. The spaces around the objects are almost as interesting as the objects themselves.

The elliptical shape effectively crops the corners of this carving titled "Dolphins" and focuses the viewer's attention on the subjects of the carving.

ellipse 10" wide by 12" tall. Get a clear plastic ruler, a pencil and two small pieces of masking tape. Use masking tape to fasten the paper to a flat surface so that the length of the paper is vertical. Then draw a vertical line up the middle of the paper. Be accurate. The line should be dead center on the width and parallel to the edges of the paper. Mark off 12" of this line and put another mark at the midway point—6". This will form the "X" axis of your ellipse.

Now draw a horizontal line across the center of your "X" axis. This line will be your "Y" axis. Measure 5" to either side of center and mark the points. These two marks determine the width of the ellipse.

Cut two small pieces of masking tape and place these at the edge of the ruler right over the 5" mark and the 6" mark. Hold the ruler up to the light so you can see the 5" mark and draw a short line on the tape at the 5" mark. Do the same for the 6" mark. This step will help you quickly identify the marks on your ruler. You'll make fewer mistakes with these marks in place. The 6" and 5" marks represent 1/2 of the "X" axis and "Y" axis respectively.

Now you are ready to draw the ellipse onto the paper. Use a sharp pencil, for the sake of accuracy. Place the ruler so that the zero mark is at the topmost point of the "X" axis. You will notice that the 6" mark is resting logically, on the center of the ellipse, which is also on the "Y" axis. As the ruler is positioned to plot the perimeter of the ellipse, the 6" mark will "slide" along the "Y" axis, just as the 5" mark will slide along the "X" axis. The zero mark will plot the perimeter of the ellipse for you. All you have to do is plot with a pencil the location of the zero mark in 1/2" increments as the 5" mark and the 6" mark slide along their respective axes.

Plot one quarter, or one quadrant, of the ellipse. No need to plot the others. If you have accurately drawn your axes, you will be able to fold the paper along the vertical axis and plot the opposite quadrant of the ellipse with the help of a light table or open window. Then, with two quadrants drawn, you can fold the paper along the horizontal axis and trace the bottom two quadrants from their counterparts in the upper half.

Now you (and I) can draw an ellipse of any size with very little frustration. Just decide how tall and how wide you want to make your ellipse. Divide each of those measurements by 2, and you're ready to start.

## Pattern Strategies

The first decision one needs to make when planning a relief pattern is the overall shape. Will it be square, rectangular, oval, round, elliptical or irregular? I've included a number of photographs to help with this first decision.

The second decision is how large to make the carving. A small carving is under 14" in width and height. A medi-

um carving is between 14" and 30" in width or height. A large carving is over 30" in either dimension. Installation carvings are the largest of them all. Sometimes they are constructed in more than one section and joined later when they are installed in a permanent setting. Other times panels for installation carvings are first constructed and fastened into place and then carved on site. These carvings can range up to several yards in width and height and might be several inches thick and weigh many hundreds of pounds.

The third decision will be whether or not to add a border. Borders can be helpful in the overall design, but they can also restrict the carving design and detract from the overall aesthetic.

I try to design patterns without borders, preferring that the pattern spill out over the boundaries of the background. If it is necessary to have a border, in order to hold a repeating pattern or text, then I prefer to place the border as deep in the carving as possible so that it does not "contain" the pattern, but rather supports it. Borders should never dominate a carving. They should not restrict, inhibit, contain or enclose a carving unless there is good reason for doing so. Their job is to enhance the carving.

Instead of borders I prefer "supporting backgrounds." An example of a supporting background is a rectangle or ellipse placed behind the other objects in the pattern and specially textured so that it provides a backdrop for the carving above it.

## Leading the Eye

Once a shape for the carving has been decided, you will want to design your pattern so it will have a point of focus. Other objects in the pattern, such as the lines that define the horizon and the foreground, should lead the viewer's eye to, not away from, the focal point. If you are, for example, carving a galloping horse, be sure to leave more space in front of the horse than behind, so that the forward motion of the horse leads the eye to the rest of the carving. If lines or layers are going to intersect in the pattern, make sure the intersection points do not cause the eye to wander away from the subject of the carving.

## Negative Space

Negative space can be defined as the empty areas around an object. Let's say you are carving a portrait of a person in cameo format. The area on the left, right, top and bottom of the portrait is considered the negative space.

Putting the correct amount of negative space in your carving is tricky at best. Too much space around a figure makes the carving look empty. Too little space around the figure makes the carving appear crowded. If there are a number of objects in a design, then the spaces between them need to be managed so that they appear balanced and well distributed. Look at the negative space in the round pattern titled "And the Two Shall Become One" (page 53) and notice how the spaces around the objects are almost as interesting as the objects themselves.

## Sources for design ideas

Did you ever have the urge to carve, only to discover, to your dismay, that you have no idea what to carve? One of the greatest obstacles—I call it a brick wall—to regular and enjoyable relief carving is developing new designs. This can be a great problem if you carve on a full-time basis. But it is also a problem for those who wait all week for their day off, so they can peacefully find refuge in carving, but instead, find themselves pacing the floor, pulling their hair, trying to think of an idea to carve.

When I first started carving 24 years ago, I used to lay awake Sunday nights, dreaming about what I was to carve on Monday, my day off. Actually, they were less dreams than nightmares, because Monday morning would find me with that empty feeling in my gut, knowing that my day off had arrived, and there was not a carving design to be found anywhere.

You might be getting the notion that finding design ideas for relief carving is not easy. Bingo! You hit the nail on the head. It takes work, organization, persistence and diligence to gather a collection of design materials that will be useful for carving.

So where do you go for design ideas? How can you avoid hitting the brick wall?

Carving ideas are like rabbits in a way. If you only have one, you will likely not get any more. But if you put two or more together, they start multiplying.

With this in mind, I have learned never to throw a design out. I keep all the pictures I have drawn—in all their preliminary stages and in all their sizes—in a file. I often re-visit my design file and find something that can be re-worked into a more successful carving. This file is now an inventory of drawings to use as resources for new carvings.

Over the years I have make it a habit to keep picture files of artwork that catches my eye. I keep files of animal photographs and drawings, and examples of artwork that deals with the human form, especially hands, faces and feet. I have a files for birds, landscapes, abstract art and religious art. All are potential sparks for a design idea.

### A word about copyright

It is important to respect the work of other artists when creating your own carving patterns. I prefer to avoid the slavish duplication of the artistic work of someone else. Instead I use their work, when appropriate, as a reference rather than as a template or pattern. That way I am able to expand, improvise and improve on their efforts as I create a unique pattern for relief carving.

Keep in mind that your growth as a carver depends on exercising your creativity and practicing proven design principles as you develop your carving patterns. You cannot do this while duplicating the work of others.

More and more I am using my camera to obtain the picture resources I need for my relief carvings. That way I am sure that I am giving my creative side the best possible workout as I move from idea to pattern to finished carving. Treat the work of other artists respectfully and respect yourself by avoiding copying.

Compression allows objects to appear closer to the viewer than other objects.

The following are some of my favorite sources for carving ideas.

### Libraries

Libraries contain lots of artwork, especially in the wildlife and art sections. Make use of the free magazines on display in the library. Search out the graphic art and advertising art sections. Often, in the reserved area of your library, you will be able to find resource books, catalogs and encyclopedias of arts and crafts. In books that catalog collector stamps or collector plates or the like, you will find a wealth of design ideas.

Translation is an important word to use here. Your carving should not be an attempt to duplicate in wood what the original artist did in his medium. Color, form and perspective have to be translated into a new medium, something that requires certain compromises and ingenuity. The result is unique.

### Magazines

Magazine stores have many publications on wildlife, geography, science, photography, the arts, sports, religion, the outdoors, design, advertising and more. Become a regular visitor to your local magazine store. The nice thing about the pictures you find there is that you can look over the magazine before you buy it.

### Advertisements

Advertisements are another great source for design ideas. Ads are everywhere, and many of them are rich in ideas. My carving students regularly bring clippings from magazines and promotional pamphlets which contain wonderfully imaginative images, which, if used judiciously, often contribute to excellent relief designs.

I always scan the newspapers and the periodicals I read at the barber shop or the dentist office for interesting images. Sometimes you will find pictures that are ready made for carving. I recently found one that showed a father, dressed in jeans and a flannel shirt, holding his infant son in his arms. Irresistible!

### Posters

Posters are another source for design ideas. Most posters contain images which, when separated from the rest of the poster design, are easily worked into a carving pattern. Stores that specialize in poster art usually carry a wide selection of posters for you to look over and catalogs of posters that they can order. They even have brochures of their posters, some of which they give out for free.

Larger objects appear to be closer to the viewer. Compare the three geese in this carving.

### Greeting Cards

Greeting cards are another easy source for carving design material. Browse through the card shops in search of floral designs, pictures of birds, decorative script, ribbons, hands, faces, animals and whatever else you need. Embossed cards even help you to understand how the design might be rendered in relief.

### Photo Calendars

Photo calendars, published yearly, offer images grouped around a particular subject, like cats, or birds or horses. These calendars brim with some of the most spectacular photography and artwork you could imagine.

### Business Cards

Business cards offer an unusual source for design ideas. You'd be surprised what good ideas come from a piece of paper 2" x 3 1/2". Business cards are usually made up of logos, which are images mixed with text. These logos are very useful for reference if you are carving a sign. They also show you how to use text, borders and various design elements efficiently and effectively.

### Other Artists

Other artists who work in stained glass or marquetry, for example, will design their projects in a way very similar to what a relief carver would. Keep your eye out for good designs. Never copy these designs outright. The idea is not to plagiarize, but to use the artwork of others as a

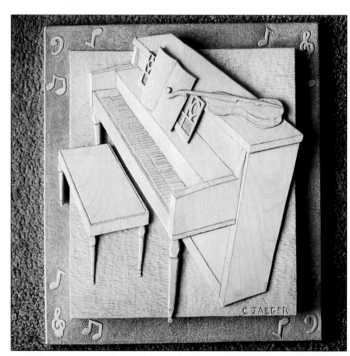

Perspective lines, such as those used in *Piano and Violin* by Clem Jaeger, help create the illusion of three "normal" dimensions.

reference, a stepping stone if you wish, for your own pattern. Never forget that what works in one medium can often work even better in wood.

### Your Camera

Your own camera is also a good source for the reference material you will use to build your next carving design. I find that I am sometimes better off taking a picture, processing it, enlarging it on a photocopier, and tracing it on my light table, than I am running around our (small) town looking for just the right image for my next carving.

A few years back I wanted to do a carving of the last supper, but I did not want to do just another rendition of Da Vinci's *Last Supper*. I wanted mine to be unique, original. So I phoned my pastor at the church and made a rush appointment to photograph him dressed in his clerical robes. I placed him behind a table in dozens of positions, and shot two rolls of 36-exposure film. I rushed down to the nearest one-hour lab and processed the pictures. Then I made enlarged photocopies and rushed home to trace these pictures onto paper.

Voila! I had 36 possible apostles, any of which could also stand in for Jesus. I laid the twelve of the best pencil tracings in a row so they looked good, placed a table in front of them, and my very own "Last Supper" was complete. The carving was a success and was well received by my customer. But most of all, it was entirely my own design. This fact alone gives me the most satisfaction.

# THE CHALLENGE OF COMPRESSION IN RELIEF

Sculptors work with the normal dimensions of width, height and depth. Relief carvers work with normal width and height, but with the dimension of depth compressed. The compression of depth presents one of the most difficult aspects of relief carving. Even though we are familiar with the relief used on common coins and medals, most of us do not know how to go about altering the depths of a relief to make it look realistic.

In relief carving, compression ratios indicate the extent to which the actual physical depth of an object is compressed, relative to the width and height of that same object. In the carving of the Malamute, which begins the gallery section of this book, I had about 9" to render the width of the wolf's head, and about 13" to render the height of the wolf's head. But I had only 1" in which to render the depth of the wolf's head. If I was to carve the Malamute in the round as a sculptor might I would need about 10" of depth. But in relief I do not have 10" of depth to work with. I must compress the depth dimension. Therefore it is easy to see that the ratio of compression for the depth has to be about 1:10.

Compression in wood reliefs can be as little as 1:2 and as much as 1:20 of the original depth of an object. If you are working in two-inch-thick panels, it is easy to see that 1:20 compression requires careful removal of the

Directional tool-marking can also give the illusion of shape and depth. Between the tip of the nose and the eyebrows there is less than 1/8" of physical depth.

wood and many thin layers in a complicated pattern. The more layers it takes to render a pattern, the flatter each of those layers is, and the more you will need to rely on directional tool-marking to achieve a sense of shape and perspective. Only the perimeters of an object are rounded over; the vast majority of the interior area being left flat. The flat areas are usually surface-textured so as to disguise their flatness.

When calculating the amount of actual depth you need for an object or layer in your relief carving, first consider how wide and tall the object is in your design, and how deep the object would be if the dimension of depth were normal. Then calculate what fraction of the actual depth is available to you for that object. That will tell you the ratio of compression.

For example, a ball is spherical and is 2" wide and 2" tall and 2" deep. But if you have only 1/4" of wood in which to carve this sphere, it will have to be compressed 1:4. This would mean that you would have about 3/16" in which to model the sphere, and another 1/16" in which to undercut the sphere, hiding the back side of it from view. Most of the sphere will be quite flat, and it will be rounded off of the sphere will be quite flat, and it will be rounded off only near the perimeter.

# EIGHT WAYS TO ACHIEVE PERSPECTIVE

Used individually or in concert, these eight ways to achieve perspective can accomplish almost all of what you desire when you attempt to create the illusion of perspective. However, there are two additional methods that I won't address here. The first is to add color to your relief. The second is to employ wood burning (pyrography). I do not use these methods myself, preferring that the beauty of the wood show through unhampered.

## 1–Overlapping Objects

When objects in a carving overlap each other, the foremost object will appear in front of all the others. This is so simple that it sometimes escapes the attention of the novice carver.

## 2–Relative Size

Used together with overlapping, relative size is the trick of scaling objects so those that are behind another object are also smaller in width and height. If you look down the road at a long line of telephone poles, the pole nearest to you will look larger than the next and so on down the line until the farthest pole appears but a dot on the horizon. You can strengthen the illusion of depth through the use of relative size: larger objects appear closer than smaller objects of the same type.

The picture of the Canada geese (page 56) illustrates this well. The goose in the foreground is scaled slightly larger than the goose behind it. The second goose has its wing tucked behind the first goose, strengthening the illusion of depth and perspective. There is a third bird, scaled much smaller, appearing in the distance. Although it is not overlapped by either of the other birds, its relative size convinces us that it is quite a distance away—even though it is only $1/2$" lower in the carving than the other birds.

## 3–Perspective Lines

Perspective lines are employed in the pencil drawing of the pattern in order to foreshorten objects, and to converge lines that are parallel in real life as they move from the foreground to the background of a pattern.

The carving, *Piano and Violin* (page 56) illustrates how effective perspective lines can be in achieving the illusion of depth and shape. This carving was taken directly from a photograph taken by the student. It was quite difficult to execute because of the flat surfaces and straight lines involved, but the illusion carries over quite well.

## 4–Actual use of depth

It seems so obvious, but it still needs to be stated that the actual rounding over (modeling) of an object helps create the illusion of depth and perspective. Block-cuts and lino-cuts (used in print making) do not use actual depth to achieve perspective, nor do V-tool carving or chip carving. Layering objects within the carving allows objects to reside at different physical levels and leaves room for objects to be rounded over.

## 5–Texturing/Detailing

Large tool marks generally suggest less detail, and since we see less detail from afar, it is appropriate to reduce detail and increase the size of tool marks as you move through to the deeper layers of your relief. Likewise, fine tool marks suggest detail, and since detail is observed only close up, the object will appear closer.

For example, a tree in the foreground should be given more detail than a tree in the background. Again, a bird close up will receive more detailed texturing and modeling than an identical bird scaled smaller, overlapped by the first and placed into a lower layer of the carving. The farther away an object is meant to appear, the less its detail will be observed.

Look at the picture of the Canada geese (page 56) again. Each of the two foreground birds has more detail on its wings than the small bird in the background. In fact the foreground birds have three ranks of feathers on their wings while the distant bird has only one. Moreover, each rank has more feathers in it than the single rank of the distant bird.

## 6–Directional tool-marking

When tool marks are directed properly, they can suggest shape and form even on a relatively flat surface. The application of fine V-tooling to represent fur on an animal is a good example of this. It would be a rather obvious mistake to carve straight parallel lines across the surface of an animal and think that the viewer will see this as hair, let alone as a realistically modeled figure. Far better to study how individual hairs lay on an animal, how they turn as they approach the perimeter of the body, how there are no parallel lines in hair, and how almost all hair follows an "S-curve" as it moves across a surface. Once the clues have been found, you are ready to cover the figure with fine tool marking.

The carving of the wolf (page 57) illustrates the effectiveness of directional tool marking. Between the tip of the nose and the eyebrows of the wolf, there is less than $1/8$" of physical depth in the wood. The entire face is essentially a flat surface that has received careful but shallow modeling and meticulous directional tool marking using a 3mm 60° V-tool. Even the ears are only $1/4$" lower than the tip of the nose.

Trees need careful texturing otherwise they will appear rigid and unrealistic. Individual boughs can be textured directionally to distinguish them from others close by. Clothing can benefit from carefully directed tool marks necessary to eliminate as much visible tool marking as possible. This way, the eye is not given more detail than necessary, and the flatness is not disguised. The surfaces of the piano in *Piano and Violin* (page 56) are an example of flat carving. Almost all evidence of toolmarking is eliminated.

## 7–Stamping

Stamping is a texture set apart from all others in the way it allows perspective to be developed in a relief carving. You can see many examples of how this texture is used in the carvings shown in this book. In the Canada geese carving (page 56), stamping is used to provide texture and contrast to the bull-rushes in the foreground.

However, stamping is most often assigned the deepest layers in a carving, usually the background itself. There it helps to clean up hard-to-get areas, especially those that are undercut. This texture absorbs light like no other texture and appears darker and deeper than surrounding wood. Being so dark it causes the layers and objects

This commission piece uses raised letters in the border and incised letters on the banner.

above it to stand out more clearly. Stamping is usually not used on foreground objects, but it can be used in tight areas that would normally gather shadow, or on borders in order to help raised text to stand out.

## 8–Undercutting

Undercutting allows a lower layer or object to be more effectively tucked under the edge of a higher layer or object. This makes overlapping even more effective. Undercutting also creates the illusion of roundness, which in itself enhances the perspective in a carving.

# USING TEXT IN YOUR DESIGNS

There are occasions when you may want to incorporate text into the design for your woodcarving.  Perhaps you wish to carve a company logo, or you have been asked to carve a family crest with your family name on it.  Or you might want to put a favorite poem or a passage into words embellished with pictures.

## Important considerations

A number of considerations need to be understood before using text in a relief carving.

*Abraham and Isaac* shows another way to combine raised and incised lettering styles.

First you need to know that whenever text is used with pictures in a relief carving, the message contained in the carving is shared between the words and the pictures. This is because feelings, ideas and sentiments can reside as much in words as in pictures. When words are carved along side of pictures, the resulting carving can often have double the impact of a carving with pictures alone.  Words change a carving from being strictly decorative or artistic into something that is much more functional. Words tap into a different layer of consciousness than pictures and evoke different, often more powerful, reactions from the viewer.

Second, a carving containing words has to be designed differently than one without. Text places certain constraints on the shape and design of the carving.  Because letters cannot be strewn all over the surface of the carving and still make sense to the viewer, the carving must be designed so that the words are placed onto the carving in an orderly, readable fashion. Text must flow from one letter to another and from one word to another along a predictable path. Thus the carving design as a whole must allow for straight, regular or evenly flowing lines along which the text can be placed.

Third, text can have a decorative function that oper-

Embossed letters, such as those used in the border of this piece, are raised only slightly higher than the surrounding surface.

ates independently of its function to inform or communicate. The carver can select from a host of text styles, called fonts, to complement the theme of the carving. The different fonts can in themselves communicate a message. For instance, Old English Script communicates a feeling of medieval antiquity. Flowing, handwritten fonts are personal and intimate.

## Drawing the letters on paper

For most people, drawing letters by hand for use in a carving design is a real pain. Even after a concerted effort, letters can end up uneven, rough and hard to read. In addition, alphabets are extremely complex, and we are used to recognizing subtle distinctions between font styles. How does one begin to draw accurate letters?

For those who have them, computers are the most helpful tools available for generating letters for use in carvings. A good object-oriented "draw" program, which has strong text handling capabilities, can generate letters in any of hundreds of typefaces and then manipulate these letters in a hundred more ways. The letters can be printed on paper, in the exact sizes and shapes that are needed, and copied to your paper design, which can then be traced to the wood. I like to print out my lettering from the computer in a straight line. I then take this line of text to the light table, where I position it accurately onto my pattern.

Computers give carvers access to typeface technology that used to be the private realm of typesetters and save many hours of work. If you don't have a computer, visit your local library and borrow a book of lettering. Many libraries now have computers for their patrons to use.

### Spelling

Check your spelling before you commit your letters to wood. Have a friend double-check your spelling, or else someday the worst will come to pass: you will finish a

carving, hang it up on the wall with pride, only to have a friend (or worse yet, a customer) point out an error in spelling. Then the only thing left to do is learn how to repair errors.

Be precise and concise when adding text to you designs. Wood is not the place to be verbose. The "KISS" principle (keep it simple, Sam) is something to always keep in mind.

## Choose a typeface

Choose the typeface that suits the theme of the carving. Old English is not suitable for a western theme, the same way Digital letters are unsuitable for carvings of flowers and landscapes. We are a literate society that unconsciously expects a lot from the written word. Subtle contradictions of theme and typeface can ruin a carving.

There are literally thousands of typefaces, each one with a particular personality. Some are quite serious, others playful, and still others are decorative. There are books on the market available for those who do not have computers, and these books contain a variety of basic typefaces. Sometimes these books provide the typeface in various sizes, as well as bold or italic. If you need to scale the letters more precisely, then you can use a photocopier to enlarge or reduce the lettering. Several of my favorite typefaces are included in Appendix A.

## Kerning

Kerning is the process of adjusting the spacing between letters to make them more readable and pleasant to the eye. The letter "L" followed by the letter "T" can look ill-spaced because of the over-abundance of space that is found between these two letters. If the space is large enough, it can even be interpreted as a space between words. You need to place these letters so that they fill their spaces more effectively. A good computer graphics program will take care of the kerning for you, but even then you may wish to kern the letters a little more.

## Special word spacers

Sometimes a carving pattern is crowded, leaving not enough space between words so that the words seem to run together, making them harder to read.

That's when "special word separators" come in handy. You can use hyphens (-) or diamonds (◊) or little bullets (•) to separate your words, thus restoring the proper spacing between words.

# STYLES OF LETTERING
## Incised letters

The most popular method of lettering for relief woodcarving is "incised lettering," that is, V-grooved letters. These letters are carved so that they are deeper than the surface of the wood. The edges of the letters slope downward to a sharp line that is located in the bottom-center of the letter. These letters are strong and, if carved with precision, very easy to read. They provide strong visual contrast, because one side of the letter will catch light while the other will be in shadow.

Incised letters are difficult to carve at first. The letters must be drawn accurately onto the wood, and then the carver has to gather the correct tools close at hand so he can switch from tool to tool rapidly. Mistakes are difficult to fix and are obvious at first glance. One has to develop a rigid and disciplined procedure for carving these letters so that there are no mistakes and no inconsistencies.

When carving incised letters, consider applying the "depth-equals-width" rule. This rule states that the deepest point of each letter should not be any deeper than the width of the widest vertical member of the letter. When incised letters are carved deeper they become harder to carve without becoming any more legible.

## Raised letters

The next most popular lettering is raised lettering, so called because the letters are higher than the surrounding wood. They may stand $1/8"-1/2"$ or more above the background, which is most often stamped in order to hide cuts and imperfections. These letters are more fragile than incised letters, and because of the tight spaces between the letters they are not always easy to carve cleanly. Raised letters are bold in appearance and very visible. It is best to carve raised letters so the sides slope outward slightly (wider at the base of the letter; narrower the top).

Sloped-sided letters carve easier and also add strength to the letters. Another benefit is the way they look "extruded" from the background. The idea is to carve the sides $1/16"$ to $1/8"$ wider at the bottom than at the top.

Raised letters under 2" tall/wide should only be about $1/4"$ higher than the background. If your letters are larger, say 3" or 4" tall/wide, then it is appropriate to raise them as much as $3/8"$ to 1" above the background. In the close-up of the carving "Abraham and Isaac" you can see both raised and incised letters being used together so that they flow from one form to the next as the underlying surfaces change.

## Embossed letters

Embossed letters are letters that have very little relief to them. They resemble the raised-relief greeting cards you often see for sale at the local card shop. Embossed letters are just a little higher than the surrounding background, which is usually stamped. What helps make them stand out from the background are beveled edges along the perimeter of each letter, a background surface that dips slightly around each letter, and the difference in texture between the smooth letters and the stamped background surrounding them.

Embossed letters are easy and quick to carve. They also occupy only a shallow range of depth within the layers of the relief carving. This means they can be applied to relatively

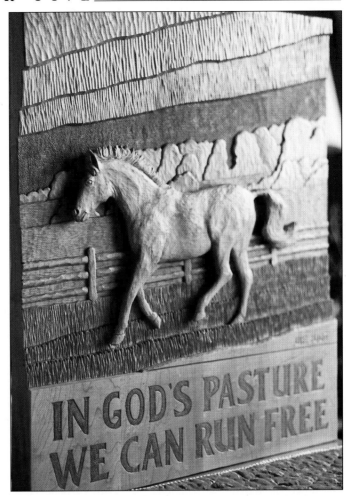

Stamped letters provide an excellent contrast against a smooth background.

shallow layers within the carving such as borders, ribbons and the like. Unlike incised and raised lettering, embossed letters do not cast large shadows. Nevertheless, properly carved, they are very visible under a wide range of viewing conditions.

## Stamped letters

Stamped letters are related to embossed letters. They are "low relief" letters whose visibility depends on bevels around the perimeter of each letter and a difference in texture between the letter and its immediate background. The feature that separates these letters from embossed letters is that embossed letters are smooth-surfaced and raised slightly above a stamped background, while stamped letters are stamp-textured and sit slightly lower than the surface of a smooth-textured foreground.

## Overlapping letters

Overlapping letters are raised letters that have been tilted so that the left side of each letter is slightly lower than the right side. This allows the left side of the first letter to the right to be tucked under the right side of the next letter, so that the first letter obscures part (just a small part) of the next letter. There are no spaces separating letters within each word, although there are spaces separating words.

## UNDERSTANDING GRAIN DIRECTION

One essential things you'll learn as you put a carving tool into wood for the first time is the proper direction for carving. Wood has grain. Grain is a directional thing. It has to be cut by a tool going in the right direction.

If you push a carving tool into the wood so that it cuts "against the grain," the wood will chip and break and splinter. Conversely, if you push a tool into the wood "with the grain," it will cut the wood cleanly and easily, leaving a polished cut behind. I have devised a simple method for explaining wood grain and proper carving direction. It is called "four quadrant carving."

### Concave shapes

Example #1 is a concave shape, like a shallow bowl, carved into the wood. The vertical axis drawn over this bowl is the direction of the grain in the wood. The horizontal axis indicates the cross-grain. These two axes divide the bowl into four quadrants. The four arrows drawn inside the bowl indicate the direction you need to carve in order to always be going "with the grain" in each of the quadrants.

Note the closely spaced parallel lines on the outside of the bowl. These indicate individual grain lines. Think of them as venetian blinds. We know that there is a right way and a wrong way to run our finger down a venetian blind. The right way, "with the grain," allows us to run our finger smoothly across the individual slats in the blind. But if we were to run our finger the wrong way, each slat in the venetian blind would catch the finger and bend out of shape.

The idea here is to think of wood grain as we would venetian blinds. The carving tool must pass over the wood grain in the right direction if it is to cut the wood cleanly. If a tool passes over the grain from the wrong direction, the tool edge will catch the grain and rip it.

Carving cross-grain, that is at roughly right angles to the grain is permissible. The wood will not rip or split, but your finished cut will not be as smooth.

### Convex shapes

Now consider example #2. This is a small sphere, rather shallow in depth as it needs to be when carved in relief. Wood has been removed around the sphere to allow the sphere to stand above the background. The convex sphere shape is the opposite of the concave bowl shape. It needs to be carved with grain direction in mind, but as you can see, the arrows point in opposite direction on the sphere. Note the closely spaced parallel lines on the surface of the sphere. Again, these represent the individual

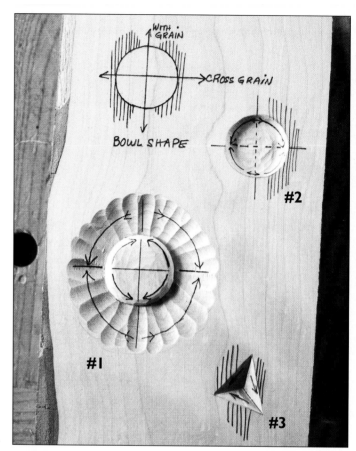

Grain direction - top view. This photo reveals the different directions one must move the tool to carve convex (raised) and concave (recessed) shapes.

fibers of grain in the wood. As the sphere is rounded, the tool needs to move in the direction of the arrows in order to cleanly and safely cut the wood. The wood that surrounds the sphere is carved essentially the same way as the bowl shape mentioned earlier.

Grain direction, side view. The division of a shape into four quadrants helps you identify where the direction for carving changes in relation to the grain

## Triangles

Example #3 is a triangle. I have not marked quadrants onto the triangle, just the closely spaced parallel lines that represent the fibers of grain and the direction they lay in the wood. Because the triangle is cut into the wood, the direction arrows are drawn on the inside walls of the triangle. Notice how the top edge of the triangle is at right angles to the direction of the grain. This means you can carve the wood in either direction safely. But the lower two sides of the triangle, need to be carved in the direction indicated by the arrows if the wood is to be cut cleanly.

# USING THE ROUTER TO SPEED WOOD REMOVAL

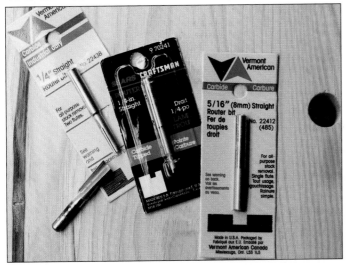

Good quality carbide router bits, though more expensive, are more durable than high-speed steel bits.

Routers help make the process of relief carving progress more quickly. They eliminate some of the "bullwork," so that a person can enjoy carving more.

Routers are generally not needed for small relief carving jobs. In fact they might cause more work than they save in some cases. But when you are working in a large panel at depths over 1/2" or on designs that have predetermined levels and large chunks of waste wood to be removed, routers make sense.

A plunge router is the only type of router to use for removing wood from a relief carving. It is called a "plunge" router because the motor and bit travel vertically on two solid metal posts, allowing the rapidly rotating bit to plunge into the wood and exit it safely.

Keep in mind that routers are initially quite expensive, as are good carbide bits. But a good router of the "plunge" variety will last decades and can be used for cabinetry and construction as well. Look for one that is around 2hp (14 amps) so that it has the power you need to router safely and cleanly.

I use the router to set the depth for the various areas

A plunge router is the only type of router to use for removing wood from a relief carving.

and levels in my carvings. A router cannot be used to effectively or safely cut slopes, so any cutting it does must be confined to removing wood to a predetermined depth, which is the highest point in a particular area of the pattern.

The deepest I go with a router is 1 1/2". This allows me to use the bits with a 1/2" shank. Because routering a relief panel must be done by hand, it is better to stay with smaller sized bits to avoid the wrenching about that larger bits can cause. Most of my relief carving is done in 2" thick panels making it unwise to router deeper than 1/2" from the bottom of the panel. The rule of thumb with router bits is that the larger the bit/shank the less suitable the router is for hand-held use. Large bits can grab a lot of wood very quickly and wrench the router out of your hands or into areas of the wood that were being reserved for hand carving.

I am more likely to make a mistake in the routering stage—either by routering into an area that I should not have or by having the router wrench out of control—than I am of making a mistake at any other stage of carving. Router mistakes are more difficult to repair, giving me even more reason to stick with the smaller bits when routering.

## Routering direction

A router bit is much like a carving tool, except that it rotates at high speed. It will cut cleaner if it is cutting the wood with the grain, rather than against it. If the bit enters the wood against the grain, it will tend to pull itself into the wood, rather than shave off the wood. Check with your router handbook for more details on the correct direction for routering.

## Routering sequence

Always router the deepest portions of the panel first. Along with this, always router inside the boundaries of an area rather than outside. When you have finished one area, move on to the next deepest area until all the routering is done. This sequence helps preserve the pattern lines of each area and layer in the carving. If you were to router from the shallowest to the deepest areas, you would find that your guide lines for the next shallowest area are being erased by the router ahead of you.

## Routering hazards

Routers can do a lot of damage very quickly, both to wood and to human flesh. I do not router wood unless my work area is safe and there are no distractions. I brace myself against the work table and the panel, so that the router is firmly in hand whenever it is cutting in the wood. I use ear protection, a mask for dust and safety glasses.

Even with these precautions, you have to ensure that the router bit does not move in the collet. If the collet is not tight enough, the bit may move outward, increasing the depth at which the bit cuts into the wood. I like to mark the bit with a felt pen close to the collet, so that I can easily see if the bit has moved in relation to the collet.

Occasionally a bit will break as a result of fatigue. When it breaks it generally just stops dead in the wood, but there is always a chance that the broken piece could fly outward. Therefore, it is imperative that plastic chip guards be used on a router.

When you are finished routering, take time to remove all the sawdust and wood chips left in the channels. Pick these out with a fine tool and use a vacuum to suck up whatever the tool leaves behind. Only when all the dust and chips are removed should you start to carve. That way the chips will not obscure the pattern or confuse you when you carve.

## Repairing accidents

As I mentioned, sooner or later the router will slip and bite out a chunk of wood that was intended to be a permanent part of the carving. When this happens, remember that a new piece of wood can be fitted to replace the damaged piece. It might take an hour to make the repair, but with care the repaired area will be invisible to the eye.

Make sure the replacement wood is of the same color and grain as the damaged site. Make sure the grain rises in the same direction. Cut out the damage wood so that you can easily glue a replacement piece of slightly larger dimension into place. Gather some sawdust from the same wood used in the panel, and mix it half-and-half with yellow glue to form a thick, moist paste. Use this paste to glue the patch into place. The paste will act as a filler for any gaps that remain between the patch and the damaged site.

## How to "waste" the wood

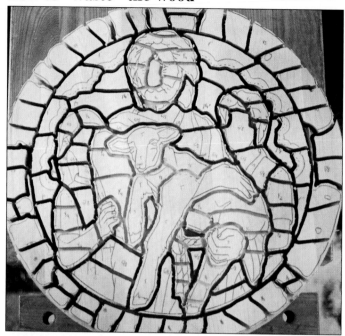

A router quickly removes wood between the sections of a relief carving.

Once routering is completed, you will have islands of waste wood to remove. This wood can be removed quickly and easily with the use of long-bent and spoon-bent gouges. The best place to start is at the deepest level of the carving, where the approach is to remove the islands of wood in three or four stages, rather than trying to chip them out with a single cut. Sometimes the wood grain will "dive" downward unexpectedly, but if you take a preliminary cut or two, you will be able to avoid taking more wood out that you intended.

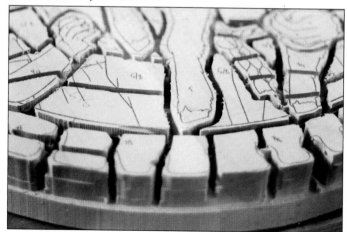

A side view of the routered relief carving shows the depth of the router cuts.

## Re-tracing the pattern lines onto your panel

When the islands of waste wood have been removed, you will have to re-draw the pattern lines onto the various

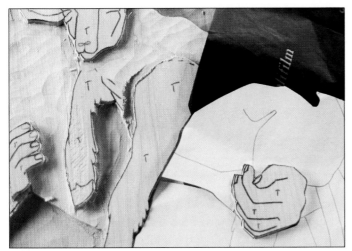

Cutting out a portion of the pattern will allow you to transfer background lines to areas where wood has been removed.

layers of the panel. I use carbon paper to transfer these lines. In addition, I photocopy my original pattern so I have copies that can be cut to fit into the lower layers of the panel. I then use carbon paper to transfer the pattern to the wood. I rarely cut my original pattern, which I keep for future reference.

Beware that you can only re-draw the lines onto one or two layers at a time. These layers then need to be carved to the lines before adjacent layers can receive their lines.

It is very important to align your pattern parts carefully when you re-draw the lines onto each area. Otherwise your pattern will "wander" and your carving will suffer.

# UNDERCUTTING
## When to undercut

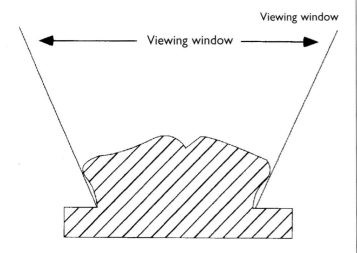

Undercutting does not begin until the surface modeling of an object is completed. For example, if you are carving a perched owl, you would first shape the owl to the point where you are ready to add details. But before starting in on the details, bevels and fine tool marking, you should cut away the sides of the object so that they are no longer visible from the front. Only when the sides of

the object are removed do you really begin to create the appearance of roundness and shape in an object. As long as the vertical sides of an object are visible to the viewer, the object appears bulky and thick.

You do not have to model all the objects and layers in the carving to undercut an object that is part of it. Sometimes it is necessary to model and undercut individual objects in order to be able to surface model those objects and layers in the carving that lie underneath. Eventually most of the objects and layers in your relief carving will need to be undercut.

## Theory of undercutting

Undercut objects appear to have roundness and realistic shape because there are no visible remnants of the original vertical sides. Consider a person standing in front of you. You can see only those surfaces of his body that are facing us. You cannot see around the perimeter of his body to see what is behind, unless he turns, in which case some of his body begins to appear while other parts disappear. If we "hide" the sides of a carved object, we are simulating what happens when we view objects in real life. When we cannot see beyond the perimeter of an object, we assume that it has a full shape, or in other words, is round.

Undercutting creates an illusion. The illusion, if well executed and coupled with accurate surface modeling of the object, will fool the viewer's eye into believing the object is fully round. However, no illusion is perfect. There is a viewing window within which the illusion holds up well. If the viewer steps too far to one side or the other, or approaches the carving to closely, the illusion may be shattered.

## Tools to use for undercutting

Although you will use a number of tools to accomplish the illusion involved in undercutting, there are a few primary tools that are most useful.

First is a #2-12mm fish-tail gouge (a similar tool is the shallow gouge you re-ground from a 1/2" carpenter's chisel). This tool will remove the bulk of the material. Because it has a shallow curve it produces a clean undercut. Overlapping cuts make for a consistently smooth shape along the edge of a figure. The fish-tail shape keeps the sides of the tool out of the way in corners and restricted spaces.

The second is a shallow #2-6mm or a 1/4" fish-tail gouge. These tools will allow you to get into tight places.

The third is a #1-12mm or a 1/2" skew with about 20 degrees of angle. These tools allows you to cut into tight corners, snipping off fibers of wood that would otherwise prevent a piece of wood from releasing.

The fourth is a #1-20mm or a 3/4" straight chisel. These tools will help you undercut larger outside curves and straight edges more effectively than a smaller tool or one with some curve to it.

Other tools will include various gouges and V-tools that you have in your collection.

## Undercut angles

Before undercutting, the sides of an object will be at 90 degrees to the background. Unless there is a specific reason for it, undercut angles do not need to be more than 75 degrees. Usually, they will be closer to 80 degrees, as this is enough to produce the illusion of roundness and to offer a wide enough viewing window to support the illusion. Undercutting at any sharper angle will not yield any benefits and will either weaken the object or make it much more difficult to clean up the background underneath.

## Keep your stop-cuts vertical

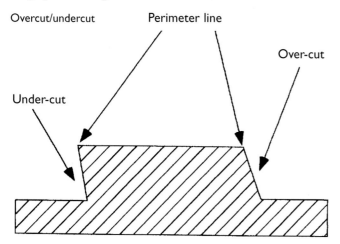

It is very important that you maintain vertical edges during the process of trimming the perimeters of objects in the carving to the line of the pattern. If your lines wander off vertical, the size and shape of the object you are outlining with your tools will start to change, introducing an amount of inaccuracy into your relief.

If your stop-cuts produce edges that are slightly overcut, that is broadening as they descend to the background, the object you are trying to outline will grow larger. On the other hand, if your stop-cuts are slightly undercut, the object will begin to shrink in size. Neither of these is desirable. Accuracy along the perimeter line is essential if you are to end up with an object that looks accurate and realistic.

## Concave undercuts are the best

The shape of the undercut edge is important to consider. Undercuts can be convex, flat or concave. Whenever possible, carve your undercut edges so they are concave. This is achieved by starting the undercut and lifting the tool handle as the cutting edge reaches the bottom of the undercut edge. Concave undercuts hide the edge of an object more effectively without having to move too far under the object.

Opposite to this is the convex undercut, formed by

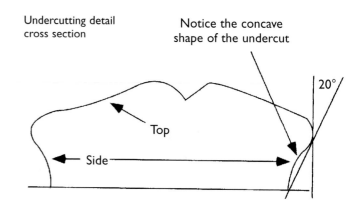

dropping the handle of the tool while the tool edge approaches the bottom of the undercut. These fail to hide the edge effectively and often cause the undercut to terminate too far under the object to allow proper cleanup of the background. Sometimes the undercut reaches far enough under the object to substantially weaken it or cause breakage.

The flat undercut is satisfactory, and in some situations the best choice, but usually it is just as easy to take the extra step to create the concave undercut.

## "Orphan" stop-cuts

When the object's perimeter is being trimmed to the tracing line, many people make the mistake of allowing their tools to cut past the bottom of the object into the background area. This mistake becomes most apparent when the object is later undercut, revealing the ugly remnant of stop-cuts now "orphaned" from the edges they once touched.

These orphan stop-cuts must either be tolerated or eliminated by removing more wood from the background behind the object. Either option is annoying, and can be easily avoided if vertical stop-cuts are terminated just above the surface directly under the object's perimeter. I usually proceed with my stop-cuts no further than 1/16" from the bottom of the edge. When it is time to undercut the perimeter these rough corners at the bottom of each edge disappear quickly.

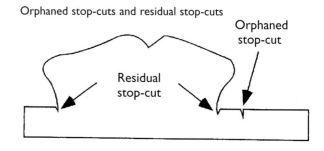

## "Residual" stop-cuts

These are different than orphaned stop-cuts only in the sense that they are desired and located where they ought to be. In order for the last fibers of wood to be removed from undercut areas, there must be some stop-cut left over. I call this a "residual" stop-cut. But residual stop-cuts are at the precise point where the undercut edge of an object meets the background. There they are out of sight and serve the purpose of allowing you remove unwanted wood chips and fibers. Residual stop-cuts will be filled with finish and virtually disappear. I have noticed that sanding sealer, my finish of preference for relief carvings, soaks into the residual stop-cuts, swelling them slightly so they close tight. After the sealer has dried, it is very hard to tell that there was a residual stop-cut.

## The Cantilever

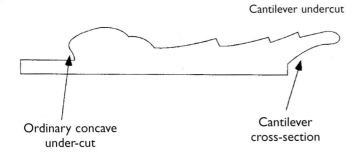

Ordinary concave under-cut

Cantilever undercut

Cantilever cross-section

A variation of the undercut is the cantilever. When an object has a part that is relatively high in respect to the underlying wood, and which sticks out, like a carved feather or wing tip or a petal on a carved flower, it is necessary that the undercut be at a sharper angle than the recommended 20-25 degrees off vertical. But when this is called for, the cantilever shape is still reasonably strong and pleasantly shaped. The strongest cantilevers are those which run the same direction as the grain.

The wing tips on the trumpeter swan are cantilevered. Notice how far they extend away from the boundary of the background.

A cantilever occurs when an object hangs over without support directly underneath it. A cantilever involves the transfer of weight to a base which is offset. Look at the photo of the trumpeter swan and notice how far out the wing tips extend from the boundary of the background. These wing tips are cantilevered. Note that the wing tip in the upper left is more closely oriented in the direction of the grain. It is stronger than the wing tip in the lower right which is oriented more in a cross-grain direction.

# USING BEVELS IN RELIEF CARVING

Types of bevels

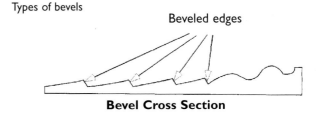

Beveled edges

**Bevel Cross Section**

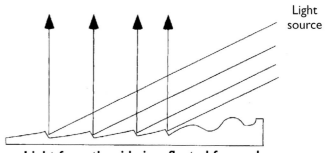

Light source

**Light from the side is reflected forward by the bevels to the viewer's eye.**

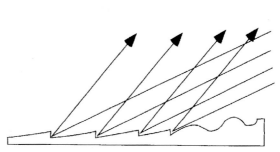

Light source

**Light from the side is reflected by the straight edges away from the viewer's eye.**

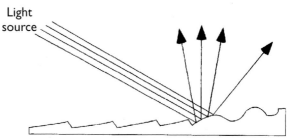

Light source

**Light from the side is scattered in many direction by a rounded edge.**

Bevels are all about catching light and shadow along the edges and perimeters of the objects and layers found in your relief carving. Without light and shadows relief carvings loose visual strength and clarity. Bevels control the light and shadows cast by the edges within the carving so that the relief is clearly visible and highly defined.

## Characteristics

Bevels are thin, single-plane surfaces applied to sharp vertical edges. Sharp vertical edges are hard to see from the normal viewing position, which is in front of the carving. This is because sharp vertical edges reflect no light, and if the edge of an object is sharp, no light is thrown out to the viewer's eye that would indicate the presence of an edge. Edges need to be seen, or else a relief carving looses definition and clarity.

This brings us to the second characteristic of a bevel: the flat plane that tilts the edge forward somewhat so that it can be seen. A 90 degree edge needs a thin 45 degree bevel. But bevels do not need to be a strict 45 degrees. They can be between 60 and 30 degrees if necessary, as long as they tilt the sharp edge forward so the viewer can see it. A 45 degree bevel is simply what is most common.

The third characteristic of a bevel is that it is not too "anything." It is not too wide, too steep, too thin or too irregular. Bevels need to be consistent, single-plane and smooth. A bevel made up of two facets, or planes, does not do as good a job defining and clarifying an edge as a single-facet bevel. This is because each facet disperses the light in different directions. A single facet delivers the light to the viewer's eye as a cohesive unit.

Bevels do not have a place on edges that are rounded over. You want to shape these edges so that they look convex-curved. The process of rounding over is actually the process of applying a collection of facets to an edge, each facet sloped at an increasing angle in relation to the previous facet. Think of a diamond ring that is modeled by facets into a round shape. A collection of facets is what constitutes "rounding over" an edge.

# WHAT TO DO WITH THE BACKGROUND
## Stamping

My favorite way to handle the deepest layer of the relief carving, otherwise known as the background, is to "stamp" it. Stamping involves striking the end of a metal tool so that the tool leaves its imprint on the surface of the wood.

Stamping has a number of excellent characteristics that make it valuable for the relief carver. First, stamping allows you to hide all those little orphaned stop-cuts, bruises and rough areas that typically end up on the background. By means of compression and controlled rotation of the stamping tool, you will be able to apply a consistent texture over a surface that was previously rough and inconsistent. Stamping also removes the reflective properties of the surface of the wood so that it appears darker than the wood above it.

## Radial tool-marking

Radial tool marking can be defined as aligning a series of tool marks so that they appear to radiate outward from a focal point somewhere in the carving. It can be applied wherever you have a relatively open and accessible background, but should not be considered where the background is crowded. The typical "cameo" format is one example of where radial tool marking is appropriate.

I like this method of texturing a background because it tends to lead the eye to the center of the carving, where the viewer finds the subject of the carving waiting to be enjoyed. Radial tool marking can be done with a broad, flat gouge or a small, tight veiner as long as the tooling is consistent and clean.

It takes a sharp tool and some practice to carve radially without leaving certain areas of the carving rough. There are four areas, located roughly at 45°, 135°, 225° and 315° (2:30, 4:30, 7:30 and 10:30 on the clock) where one side of each tool mark will cut clean while the other side will cut rough. In these four areas, I carve the rough side of each radial tool mark from the opposite direction

Bevels catch light along edges, adding definition and highlights. The raised letters are beveled on their edges, as are the large feathers on the rooster's neck and the edges of the ribbon and the borders.

The background is tool marked in an attractive radial pattern.

in order to get rid of the rough wood. The extra work is worth it though, as this method of texturing adds drama and focus to your relief.

## Smooth tool-marking

Of course, backgrounds can be tool marked smooth,

A combination of smooth and cross-grained tool marking is featured on the background of this carving.

as long as they are reasonably accessible. The smoother the surface, the brighter it will appear compared with the wood above it. If the background is carved smoothly enough, you will be able to clearly see the grain pattern in the wood.

## Cross-grain tool-marking

Finally, you can use a #5-10mm or a #7-10mm gouge to cut grooves directly across the grain over the entire background. Like stamping, cross-grain tool marking provides you with a consistent and controlled surface, helping you to carve out defects, stop-cuts and the like. Use this technique on a background that is relatively open and accessible.

# TIPS FOR CARVING LETTERS

First, accuracy is essential in carved letters. Make sure your spelling is correct. I have on occasion failed to pick out errors in spelling that were noticed later by my wife, fortunately in time for me to correct them before delivering the carving to my customer. How embarrassing!

Second, make sure that your letters are accurately and consistently drawn on paper, and later, on the wood. Use fresh carbon paper and a sharp pencil to transfer the letters from the paper design to the wood. Otherwise the lines of the letters will be too faint or too vague for accurate carving to take place.

Third, practice an unfamiliar style of lettering on a spare piece of wood, to give yourself time to adjust your hands, mind and tools to what you are attempting to do.

## Wasting wood

Wasting wood with a router is a practical way to speed up the process when carving raised text. Sometimes I space the letters so I can fit a 1/4" straight router bit between them. This allows me to router an even depth of background around the letters, and opens a space that makes it easy to carve the sides of each letter. I use a "plunge router" because ordinary routers are hard to use in such tight spaces. A plunge router will let you move the spinning bit in and out of the wood with great precision, reducing the risk of accidentally damaging the carving. I usually carve spaces that are too tight for a 1/4" bit by hand. Smaller bits are hard to control and usually burn the wood.

## Stamping

Stamping the background around raised letters is almost always the way to go. Stamping darkens the background, covers up all the cuts and irregularities that exists there, and generally tidies things up a lot.

## Tooling

Tooling the surface of the letters is usually better than sanding. Tool-marks, especially those made with very sharp tools, produce smooth and shiny surfaces, with a clear, deep color. The textured surface also reflects light in a more pleasing fashion. If, however, you choose to sand the letters (and there are times when this is the correct way to go), be sure that you do not need to do any more carving with your tools. Particles from the sandpaper lodge in the wood and will dull the sharp edges your tools with amazing efficiency.

## Bevels

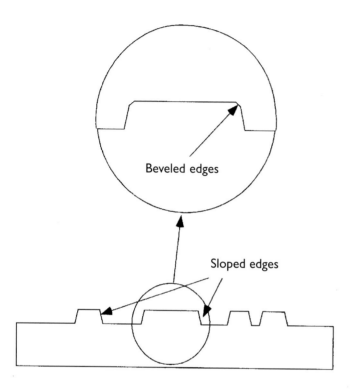

Raised letters have sloped edges to strengthen them and give them the "extruded" look. Adding bevels gives the letters more clarity.

Bevels are the last thing you have to do to complete the lettering. They are important if you wish to produce letters that are clean-edged and readily visible to the viewer. Bevels (called chamfers) are narrow, flat surfaces applied at a 45° angle to the edge of each letter. They serve two purposes: first, they replace ragged edges with smooth-cut edges, and second, they make each letter more visible to the viewer.

## MISCELLANEOUS TIPS AND TECHNIQUES
### Burnishing Tool

Burnishing is the process of rubbing parts of the carving with a hard, polished piece of wood, such as hard maple. It is done after all the tooling is completed, and just prior to applying the finish. When the smooth piece of maple is rubbed hard over the surface, it tends to compress the carved surface slightly and to raise its sheen as well. Some of the crisp edges of the tool marks are flattened, leaving the surface that is burnished looking softer and more reflective than the un-burnished wood around it.

A burnishing tool will compress the carved surface slightly and make it shiny.

I use burnishing as an alternative to sanding when I want a surface to look soft and smooth. Burnishing works well on a face or a hand to visually separate it from the surrounding surfaces. Sometimes the entire carving is burnished in order to raise its reflective values. Keep in mind that burnishing compresses wood and, in the process, erases fine detail. Use this technique only if this is what you want to accomplish.

Surface carving with a veiner produces a simple but effective result.

### Surface Carving with a Veiner

Sometimes surface carving is all that is needed in order to convey a simple message through your relief. I use a 12-2mm or 12-3mm veiner to carve simple lines on an otherwise flat surface. The result is similar to a thick line drawing. The veiner allows you to carve without regard to the grain of the wood, as long as you keep the shoulders of the cutting edge out of the wood, and you can

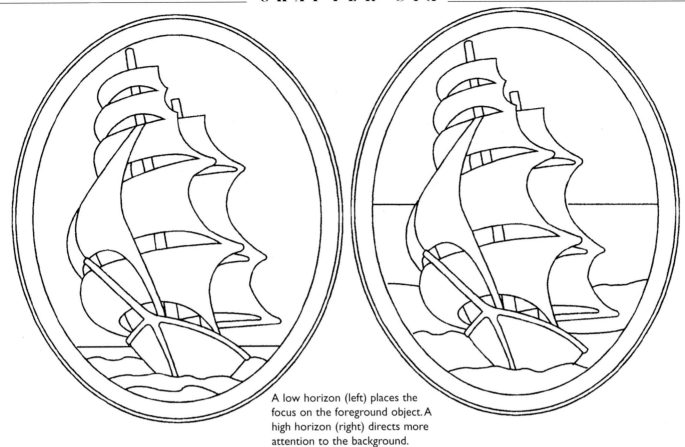

A low horizon (left) places the focus on the foreground object. A high horizon (right) directs more attention to the background.

carve any direction.

Make sure the surface to be carved is perfectly flat and smooth, without scratches or flaws of any sort to distract from the carving. A V-tool is also useful for this type of surface carving, but the resulting line is not as soft in appearance as that produced by the veiner.

## Where to place the horizon

Whenever your carving pattern includes the use of a horizon, as it would if you were carving a landscape, you need to decide precisely where that horizon is to be placed. A low horizon makes the subject stand alone in the foreground and dominate the scene. The landscape itself has diminished importance. However, a high horizon gives the landscape a higher status in the overall carving, bringing it into the foreground to compete with the subject for attention. In the same way, a low horizon implies that the viewer is at the same level as the subject of the scene; a high horizon implies that the viewer has a more elevated view of the scene.

## Basket weave

This is an unusual but attractive form of background decoration. It commands the attention of the viewer and should be used only where it will not distract from the subject of the carving. Basket weave requires more planning and measurement than other forms of background texturing or decoration.

Basket weave is not suitable for tight spaces. Its best application is on plain, open backgrounds that would oth-

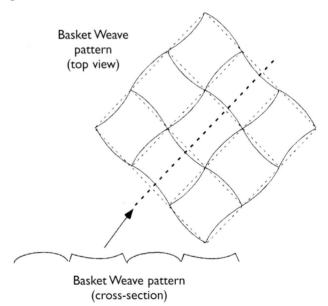

Basket Weave pattern (top view)

Basket Weave pattern (cross-section)

erwise look bare and uninteresting. The axes of the basket weave need to be drawn at 45 degrees off vertical so that all four sides of each square of the weave will gather flattering shadows and be easily visible.

Basket weave is a repeating pattern and needs to be drawn and carved carefully and consistently. It is a good idea to experiment on a scrap piece of hardwood prior to attempting it on an actual carving. You must carve a number of weaves before you develop a regular and consistent approach to carving the individual basket weaves.

Recently I was commissioned to create a carving based on the Biblical parable of the "Prodigal Son" from Luke 15: 11-24.

The family who commissioned the carving chose this particular theme because it clearly portrayed the compassion of God within the actions of the father of the prodigal lad. This was the same quality of compassion the parents desired to display towards their children and teach their children to emulate. Having known this family for nearly 25 years, I have seen this type of compassion in action in their home, so it was clear that this carving was meant to testify to compassion being central to the family belief system.

The idea was also to create a "family heirloom" which would have enduring meaning to the family over successive generations. Artistic considerations were to take a back seat to the message of this carving. It had a job to do, and if it were to look aesthetically pleasing in the process, all the better. What good would the carving be if it looked pretty but failed to communicate the central belief of the family or the essence of this parable?

I focused on verse 20 because this is where the compassion of God (the father) is most clearly identified in the parable. It was important to capture the moment that the father first saw his son returning home, and the joy that would be displayed in his eyes and on his face. His hands are clasped close to his breast in grateful celebration and anticipation.

For the carving to effectively present the father's joy in context, it was necessary to incorporate the actual text of verse 20 as well as scenes from the rest of the story. Thus, the lad is first shown in the pig pen, distraught because of what he had become. Next the lad is shown heading home, resolved in his heart to admit his sin and beg for mercy. Finally, the son meets his father, who, overjoyed at the son's return, embraces him and restores him to full sonship again. The presence of God, represented by the rays starting in the upper left, form the background over which the scenes are portrayed.

The father is the most detailed object in the carving, followed by the text of verse 20 and finally by the line carving around the perimeter of the ellipse.

The carving is 2" thick and 18" by 24", carved in Northern white birch, with a clear finish (sanding sealer/wax).

**1** One of my carving students has a substantial beard and the face shape that has potential to become an elder Hebrew father typical of the time when this parable was first told. I traced the photos and then "aged" the face so that it was to my liking. The hands came from another photo.

**2** The "aged" drawing was further enlarged 150% using a pantograph rather than a photocopier. This gave me a scaled pencil drawing that could be further edited using pencil and eraser.

**3** I drew an ellipse (left) using the "trammel" method (see page 52) to the exact size I needed to encircle the image of the father. An ellipse allowed me to crop the corners of the image tightly.

**4** On the computer, I generated the text that I used in the carving. I produced the text in a straight line, even though my graphic program will allow me to wrap text around an ellipse. I prefer to trace lettering by hand, making minor adjustments as I go. The three peripheral drawings were drawn to scale in preparation for tracing them into the full-sized pattern.

**5** The full-sized pattern now contains all the components and details that will appear in the final carving. The more accurate the final pattern is, the more accurate the final carving will be. Depth markings have been added to the pattern in preparation for routering. Shaded areas will be textured with stamping.

**6** I cut boards to length in preparation for planing to thickness and jointing the edges. This is what white birch looks like in its rough lumber form. Behind the boards is a lift of white birch slowly seasoning in my shop. What a "gold mine!"

**7** The boards have been planed to thickness and jointed on their edges. The photo shows the boards stacked on edge, where I examine them for accuracy in the joints. No light should show through the joints or else the joints will be weak and unsightly. Notice that the panel shows some camber (cupping).

**8** The prepared boards are placed in proper sequence according to the rise of the grain and general appearance. Glue is applied and the clamps are tightened. Make sure the shop is warm at floor level, or else raise the clamped panel up onto a bench where the air is warmer. The glue will fail to "knit" properly if the shop is colder than 50°F (10°C).

**9** Here the pattern was traced onto the panel using carbon paper. Then the perimeter of the panel was bandsawed to the line. I usually go over the carbon-paper lines with a dark pencil to make sure they are clearly defined. This makes it easier to router the panel accurately and safely later on.

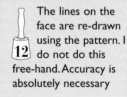

**10** Routering is accomplished with a sturdy Makita 2hp plunge router. This stage takes total concentration and a firm grip on the router. I use a $3/8$" carbide bit, which allows me to go as deep as $1 1/8$" into the panel. Ear protection and a dust mask are essential. All the saw dust is removed completely before I proceed with removing the islands of wood left by the router. These islands are removed with hand tools.

**11** This is what the panel looks like after all the routered areas have been roughed out to their proper levels. Most of the original tracing lines have been lost, but they will be replaced, one level at a time, as the carving progresses.

**12** The lines on the face are re-drawn using the pattern. I do not do this free-hand. Accuracy is absolutely necessary

**13** The eyes are modeled next. All I want to do at this point is get them modeled. The fine details will be added later.

**14** When the figure is completely modeled I cut my original pattern and place it over the ellipse, which acts as a guide to "register" the pattern correctly. The text is then traced onto the panel using carbon paper.

**15** Here is what it looks like when the letters have been completely re-traced onto the carving.

**16** I use a V-tool to rough out the letters. It is easiest to rough out two or three words at a time, to avoid having to swap tools all the time.

**18** In this photo the carving has been completely carved but has not yet received the finish. I tend to be a "clean" carver, eliminating all fuzzy or rough areas. The photo of the finished piece appears at the beginning of this section on page 72.

**17** Here the letters are carved but not yet surfaced. Notice that the stamping has already been done around the letters. Stamping helps to clean up the area around the letters and help to display them better.

RELIEF ◆ CARVING

# FINISHING ALTERNATIVES

## SANDING YOUR CARVING

The word "sanding" is known among my carving students as the "S" word. Sanding, and the mention of it, should be avoided in relief carving. There is nothing that sanding does to wood that sharp carving tools and a little technique can't accomplish far better.

If someone says they want a really smooth surface on the wood, I tell them that sharp tools leave a surface far smoother and shinier than sanding can achieve. If they tell me that they want to get rid of chips and fuzzies, I tell them that it is better to carve these out.

Sanding dulls carved wood. It is as simple as that. It takes the crisp edges of individual tool marks and erodes them into rounded and insipid ridges that fail to catch light and shadow. Sanding destroys the light-reflecting

Scrapers and sharp tools are preferred over sandpaper to make a carving: "smooth."

properties of a crisp tool-marked surface. Sanding leaves behind millions of particles of abrasive that will quickly dull any tool. Sanding scratches the surface so that the application of stain highlights these blemishes. If these reasons are not enough, then add to them the fact that sanding is hard to do especially when there are tight corners with which to contend.

Those who are most likely to use sanding are those who cannot (yet) manipulate their tools effectively to model and tool mark an object. But there are also those who need to resort to sanding because their tools are dull and rough, causing the wood to chip and break, and leaving "tracer marks" over the surface of the tool cuts. It is better to learn how to use and sharpen your tools proper-

ly. Carving tools are so versatile in the first place that they make sandpaper totally unnecessary.

An alternative to sanding is the scraper. A good wood scraper, properly sharpened and skillfully used is not much different than a carving tool, because a scraper cuts the wood with its sharp hooked edge while it is dragged across the wood. Scrapers allow a carver to level a flat surface quickly because the average scraper is much wider and flatter than most carving tools. Sometimes it is necessary to leave a surface with no visible tool marking. This is something a scraper does well.

Smaller narrow scrapers can be made from old hacksaw blades. These allow you to scrape in tight areas and to smooth convex surfaces.

## THE FINAL DECISION

You've spent dozens of hours laboring over a relief panel, carving a unique gift for a special person in your life. The last chip of wood has been removed, and finally you can apply the finish to the carving. But what finish should you put onto your relief? Here is a list of finishes that work well.

Oil
Beeswax
Tung oil
Varethane
Urethane
Paint
Stain
Shoe polish
Lacquer

### Oils

(Rating: poor) All oils and oil-based products, with the exception of Tung oil, basically do the same thing. They apply easily, soak into the wood, and allow for subsequent re-coats to achieve the desired gloss. They are safer to use than a lot of products, but when it comes to relief carving in particular, they pose some definite disadvantages.

First and foremost, oils take a lot of time to apply, especially in larger reliefs. A number of coats need to be applied to achieve a suitable "satin" sheen. Each coat takes at least overnight to dry, and the grain is raised with each coat, requiring the application of some steel-wool and elbow grease to smooth the wood prior to re-coating.

Second, the sheen is very difficult to control on a carved surface where the end-grain gobbles up many times more oil than the flat grain. As a result, the relief carving will be shiny in one spot and dull in another. The finish you want for your relief should leave the carving with perfectly consistent reflective values over its entire surface.

Third, oils tend to temporarily soften large relief panels, so that they cup toward the carved side even more than they normally would. The result is a carving that is dimensionally distorted, unattractive and hard to hang on the wall.

## Beeswax

(Rating: poor) Normally, beeswax would be applied by hand-rubbing it into the wood. The result is a soft, even glow over the entire carving. And it smells so good too! But how do you get the wax into the tight areas, like into corners and under the undercutting? And forget about applying it over a stamped surface. Forget also about bringing out the natural beauty of the grain, because beeswax does not soak in. It sits on top of the wood. Leave beeswax to the wood turners where it belongs.

## Tung Oil™

(Rating: good, but limited usefulness) Tung oil can produce an attractive, durable, beautiful finish on a woodcarving, as long as you are not trying to apply it to stamped areas, undercutting, and rough-textured areas. Tung Oil™ is a time consuming finish to apply, each coat building on the other until the sheen is just right. It is applied sparingly, so there is no problem with softening the relief panel as with other oils. However, Tung Oil is only suitable for very smooth relief carvings that can be hand-rubbed. Best to keep the panel small too, or you will have to watch a lot of TV while applying the finish, just to keep from going stir-crazy.

## Varethane/Urethane

(Rating: poor) Varethanes/urethanes were designed for the furniture/flooring industries to be a hard, durable finish, suitable for daily wear and tear and foot-traffic. Because they are so hard, you cannot apply them to your relief and then expect to easily remove imbedded particles and brush-hairs. Neither can you expect to avoid runs and puddling. These products don't soak into the wood; they sit on top of the wood, making the wood look like it was coated with plastic. Leave these products for use on your furniture and hardwood floors.

## Paint

(Rating: good) The right paint could look really nice on a carving. The right paint can soak into the wood just enough to bind with the surface, but not enough to hide delicate textures. Some paints are semi-transparent and allow the grain to show through. The problem with paint, however, is that it hides the natural reflective properties, the color and the figure of the wood it sits on. If you have used a cheap wood for your carving, this what you want

the paint to do, because paint will hide defects.

Another advantage is that color can add to the beauty and meaning of a relief carving. Many cultures demand that carvings be painted as a matter of course. Be careful to ensure that the appearance and functionality of your carving will be enhanced, not diminished, by the paint you plan to apply.

This having been said, color can also ruin a carving quite easily. Consider attempting to carve a relief portrait of a relative. In order to achieve realism, it is necessary to do more than use one color for the skin and another for the hair and a third for the clothing. The process of achieving realistic skin color is a complex thing, and hair is never one shade only but a blend of lights and darks. Reducing the appearance of objects to colors that are too simple ends up looking quite primitive and childish and competes with the relief for visibility.

Properly used, however, color, can work together with relief and texture to produce a desirable effect. Choose your paint wisely. Apply it only after testing it carefully on a "sample" carving. Get the expert advice of an experienced carver who has used paint in the past. And pray that it works out.

## Shoe Polish

(Rating: good-very good) Shoe polishes (I use the newer "shoe creams" that are on the market) contain a heavy measure of pigment, in a multitude of colors, suspended in a soft wax paste. I apply them with a tooth brush and use a clean bristle brush followed by a soft cloth to buff. The result is a soft, even finish over the entire carving.

Advantages of this finish are many. It is a one-step finish. It is easy and fast to apply. As long as you make sure that none of the polish dries before you have a chance to brush it out, and you are careful to clean excess polish from corners and cracks, this product is hard to misuse.

Unknown to many, polish is imbedded onto the surface of your relief unevenly. This means that on flat grain little of it adheres, leaving the wood to show through more. On more porous cross-grain and end-grain, polish adheres more heavily, making the wood look darker or more colorful. This is not a problem because the differences in surface adhesion make for subtle gradations of color intensity over the carving, with some surprisingly beautiful effects.

Polish also tends to hide defects, like the color differences between pieces of wood that are glued side by side and mineral streaks that sometimes appear in the most awkward places in a carving. If the wood will not look absolutely beautiful with a clear finish, then use your favorite shoe polish. But try the polish on a spare piece of relief carving first, just to get the hang of it.

## Liquid Stain

(Rating: poor-good) Stains can turn your carving into

an instant disaster. They soak into the open grain, and wipe off the closed grain, leaving all but the closest grained woods streaked, striped, blotchy and ugly. Never use stain on a relief carved in oak, ash, elm or similar coarse-grained woods. Woods like hard maple and basswood can receive stain, as long as the stain is diluted. Basswood needs to be conditioned first, otherwise it will absorb the stain unevenly.

The problem is what to put on top of the stain to give the carving a soft glow. Many top-coat finishes will dissolve the stain as they are applied and make a terrible mess. Spray finishes can be applied as long as they are compatible with the stain. Most carvers will not want to take the time to learn the chemistry or want to take the risk of messing with stains. Those that do will learn from their mistakes.

Wood conditioning products are designed to prepare softwoods to receive stain. Their purpose is to condition softwood so that it absorbs the stain evenly, without blotchiness. But I know of no product that will condition porous hardwoods, like oak, ash and elm, and the porous end-cuts that are always abundant in a relief carving.

## Lacquers

(Rating: fair-good) Lacquers can work very well on a relief woodcarving. They can be applied in multiple coats, and produce a controlled, usually "soft" appearance. If applied correctly, lacquers will enable you to produce a drip and streak-free finish. But lacquers are very difficult to master and require expensive equipment or spray cans to use. In addition, you need to protect your lungs with expensive respirators. And don't forget the explosive nature of the vapors that come off these lacquers. Lacquers also require a dust-free environment to keep dust particles from being embedded into the finish.

## The SSW Method

(Rating: excellent) "Sanding Sealer/Wax" is by far the best finish I have ever used. It involves a base-coat of quick-drying sanding sealer, followed by '000' steel wool to smooth the surface, and finally a top-coat of hardwood floor paste wax. This is a finish that I discovered in my studio and which I have had the pleasure of sharing with other carvers for many years.

Sanding sealer is a specialty product that is available in many paint stores. It is applied to relief carvings with a brush, soaks into the wood and dries to the touch in ten minutes (re-coats in 4-6 hours). It effectively seals the wood and brings out the wood's inner beauty. Sanding sealer is a clear finish.

Because sanding sealer soaks in, it does not puddle in low spots, corners and tight places. Because it is a soft finish, any runs can be removed with steel wool prior to applying a wax topcoat.

By itself, sanding sealer is absorbed into the wood unevenly, depending how porous the wood is. The result is that your relief carving, with only sanding sealer on it, will look rather unevenly finished. Some parts will be shiny and others will look flat.

This is where the steel wool comes in. Take '000' steel wool and evenly rub the entire carving (except, perhaps very rough or stamped areas) until all dust particles stuck in the finish are removed, along with brush hairs and the like. The idea is to scuff the sanding sealer evenly, in preparation for the application of the paste wax. Paste wax is what puts the shine back onto the relief carving.

Apply the sanding sealer evenly over the carving: back first, then sides, then the front. Let the finish dry overnight. Steel-wool the carving the next day, taking care to be vigorous enough to remove imperfections like dust particles and runs, but not so vigorous as to remove wood or erode the toolmarking. Then, vacuum and wipe the carving thoroughly, so there is no trace of dust, steel-wool particles or grit remaining.

Go over the carving once more, using your finger nail or a small metal pick, to remove any remaining particles and imperfections in the surface finish. Then apply an even (not thick) coat of paste wax (suitable for hardwood floors... not liquid wax) over the areas that you scuffed with the steel wool. Use a soft cloth to apply the wax. Buff the wax with a pure, soft, bristle brush, removing any excess wax from cracks and corners. Finally, use a clean, soft cloth to polish the carving until it shines. The result will be a soft, even, smooth-to-the-touch finish that will be the envy of your carving colleagues.

This finish will invite touching, but don't worry, because the top-coat of wax resists finger prints. Let people touch the carving to feel how smooth the surface of your carving is. To clean your carving in the years ahead simply vacuum the carving with a soft brush attachment, and wipe with a soft, dry cloth. Do not re-apply wax, especially spray waxes. Do not use a damp cloth to dust your carving. This finish is durable, maintenance free and designed to last for decades.

## PROPER LIGHTING FOR RELIEF CARVING

The phrase "put it in the most favorable light" describes perfectly the way to present and illuminate relief carvings. A relief requires controlled lighting in order to look its best, and part of the lighting decision is the decision of where to hang it.

Light crosses the carving and casts shadows that make it possible for the viewer to actually see the features of the relief. Without shadows it is difficult to see detail and depth and texturing. Relief carvings need light from the side if the boards in it are oriented vertically, and from the top if the boards in the panel are oriented horizontally. Light from the front of the carving is the least desirable.

Many carvers do not realize that when they take their carvings to a local carving show, where the carvings will be viewed laying flat on a table in a large room with overhead florescent lights, they are presenting their carvings in the worst possible light. The face of the carving is directly facing the light source, and thus there are few, if any, shadows to highlight the relief. In addition, the light in that situation causes the natural beauty and reflectivity of the wood to disappear.

Most art galleries are also poor places to hang carvings for display. This is because the system of "raked" lighting throws light onto the carving from angles that are too far forward and from too many angles. Carvings visually "wilt" in light that would otherwise bring out the best in a print, water color or oil painting.

### Types of lighting

Natural light is by far the best light for viewing relief carvings, especially if the window providing the light is at right angles to both the wall on which the relief carving is hung and the orientation of the individual boards in the relief panel.

A large picture window, and even a smaller bedroom window allows far more light to enter a room during the day than can be provided by most artificial lights. Natural light is "full spectrum" and able to bring out the natural beauty of the wood.

However, evening lighting is an important consideration too. Artificial lights should not be placed in front of a relief carving, but rather to the side, a short distance away from the carving. You need to check the effect of artificial light on a carving prior to mounting the carving on he wall. Have someone hold the carving in the spot you would like it to hang, and check to see that the carving

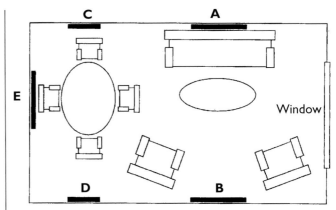

A and B - The best locations, strongest light/shadow. C and D - Acceptable locations, weaker light/shadow. E - Acceptable locations, carving seen by reflected light

shows well. You should be able to see all the detail, and the shadows cast by the light should not obscure detail.

If the carving does not show well, move it to another location. Because I work at home, I like my carvings to look best during the daylight hours, and I am willing to put up with less-than-best lighting during the evening hours. Someone who is home only in the evenings will prefer to have artificial lights provide the best lighting.

Unfortunately, artificial lights always fall short of natural light. Either they are not as bright, the light they offer is too one-directional, or they distort the colors of the wood to some degree. Halogen lights are better than ordinary incandescent bulbs, which are better by far than florescent tubes.

Light that crosses a relief panel parallel to the orientation of the boards is also less desirable. The angle and intensity of the light may be correct, but much of the light will be absorbed by the wood, instead of being reflected back to the viewer. It seems wood will allow light to enter the grain and be swallowed up by it unless the light crosses the grain at right angles. Then it is reflected forward for the viewer to see, and reveals the grain and the color, as well as the relief, texture and detailing.

## HANGING YOUR CARVING
### Visual weight

Over the years I have heard many potential customers tell me that they do not want a carving that is too large. When I ask "What is too large?" they usually cannot define this in specific terms. So I ask them if "too large" is the size of a small framed painting, a medium framed painting or a large framed painting. As I ask them this, I hold my arms out to indicate size. Usually they say "too large" means larger than a medium framed painting. When I show them that the average relief carving in the home is between a small and a medium sized framed painting, they are quite surprised, and quickly acknowledge that they thought most carvings were larger.

I share this observation in order to point out that relief carvings are perceived as being larger than they actually are. It has to do with their visual weight. Even a medium-large relief carving measuring 22" x 32" is smaller than a medium-sized painting. But because it is thick and has relief to it, it looks larger.

When you estimate the size of carving for a particular space on the wall of a home, find a picture about the correct size for the space and take its measurements. A relief carving of the same dimensions will fit in that space just as well. You'll find that most walls are large enough for a medium-large relief carving.

## Hanging Small Carvings

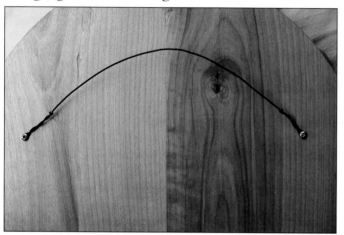

Two screws and single-strand wire are used to hang carvings.

Almost all of my reliefs are hung on a 4" nail driven at a slight downward angle into a wall stud. On masonry walls you might use a screw fastened into an anchor. On the back of the carving I have installed two screws and a strong, single strand-wire (such as bailing wire or a coat hanger). The apex of the wire should not be closer than 1 1/2" from the top of the carving so that it and the nail in the wall will be well hidden.

It is important to avoid using multi-strand wire, as individual strands eventually break, weakening the wire. Bailing wire, on the other hand, is tough, inexpensive and easy to use. When the carving is hung, the wire holds its shape. I wind this wire around the screws so that it cannot be pulled off. Then I twist the screws firmly into the wood.

The screws must be inserted into pre-drilled holes in most hardwoods so that they do not twist off when being turned into the wood, and so the wood does not crack from the expansion of the screw. Drilling into the back of a carving can be a little worrisome, so I estimate the thickness of the wood available at the point where I wish to place the screw, and then place some masking tape on the appropriately sized drill bit to indicate how deep the drill should go.

Some houses have plaster-board (gyproc) walls, which by themselves are unable to support the weight of even the smaller carvings. To hang larger carvings, drive a nail into a wooden stud. A 4" nail driven into a stud to within 3/8" of the wall surface will hold a 50 pound carving quite easily. If the carving is wide enough that is easily spans two studs, then is better yet to use two nails to hang the carving.

## Hanging large carvings

My definition of a large carvings is one that is more than six square feet in area. Carvings of this size need a stronger hanger than wire, screws and a nail.

I prefer to construct a two-piece wooden hanger, where the first piece is fastened by screws to the back of the carving and the other to the supporting wall. This hanger takes more time to construct, but will allow you to hang large carvings with confidence. Because the carving merely rests on the wall and is not fastened directly to it, this system allows the carving to "move" as humidity changes in the house.

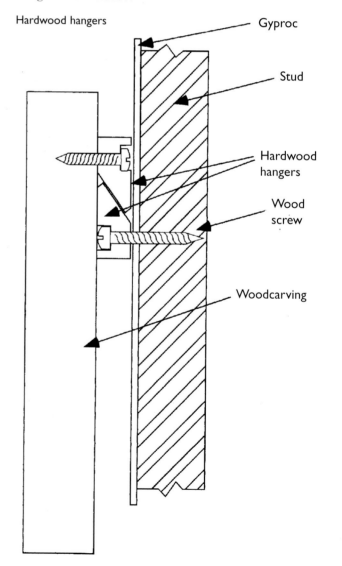

Hardwood hangers

Gyproc

Stud

Hardwood hangers

Wood screw

Wood screw

Woodcarving

## PROMOTING YOUR WORK

If you plan to supplement your income from carving sales and instruction, you'll want to read this chapter carefully. Considerable thought, time and effort go into showing your carvings and building a reputation. I'd like to share with you some tips on how to promote yourself and your work.

### Galleries

Public art galleries—especially formal galleries where carving is most often seen as "folk art" or "primitive art"—may not be the best place to show your work. Galleries generally have a board of directors that oversee day-to-day operations and a curator who has earned an art degree. Often there is a process of submission for anyone wishing to show his work in the gallery, and the criteria may prevent un-recognized artists from having a show.

Public art galleries are also not set up for relief carving. The lighting was installed to illuminate pictures and prints, and perhaps the occasional sculpture. Many times there is a commission charged on the sale of items that are displayed at the gallery. This is reasonable enough in principle, but may be costly if the commissions are over 20% of the sale price.

Private galleries are another matter. Most charge between 30% and 50% of sales and ask for exclusive rights to an artist's work before they will agree to be "agents" for the artist. Some artists prefer dealing with private galleries because they do not have to hunt down sales opportunities for themselves. If you can produce carvings quickly and cheaply so that they are still affordable after the gallery markup has been added, then private galleries might be an option for you. But most relief carvers invest so much time in their carvings that they are unable to earn a reasonable wage for their time, especially when the buying public is not well informed about the value of woodcarving in the first place. If the price of a carving is inflated to allow for commissions of 30-50%, it soon becomes out of reach to all but the most affluent customers.

### Exhibitions

Local fairs and craft shows are better suited to showing your carvings because they draw from the general public rather than a smaller elite art community. Many communities have annual craft shows or art/craft competitions where there is little cost involved in showing your work. These events often allow you to control the way your work is displayed, which is important if your carvings are to look their best. They also allow the artist to be present to meet the viewing public and promote his work directly.

The people that run these events are sometimes paid but are more often volunteers who love their work and do a fine job drawing the community to these events, while at the same time, attending to those who display their work. The spirit of service and volunteerism at these events is often high and makes for a healthy environment in which to promote yourself and your work.

### Commercial craft shows

These are highly promoted events structured primarily to make a profit for the promoter and secondarily to provide the craftsperson and artist with a means of making a living. These are expensive events that cost the participants dearly. Only those who are sure that they will be able to sell enough to make it worth their while should participate. All too often these events leave a sour taste in the mouths of the struggling artists and craftspeople who have lost money by participating in them. No matter what the promoter promises and claims, seek out people who have attended these events to find out if it was worthwhile for them. Only then can you confidently commit yourself to the time and expense of being involved in a commercial craft show.

### Fund raising events

These events raise money in a number of ways. Some charge admission while others charge a percentage of sales. Some charge using a combination of both admission fees and percentage of sales. There is a third category of fundraiser that asks for donations of artwork from artists who are in return given publicity and a generous tax receipt for their contribution. In some cases the "donation" scenario offers good exposure in comparison to the costs incurred by the artist.

Fund raisers are aware that artists need to find these events worthwhile or they will not participate. Without participation from the artists no funds can be raised. As a result, artists will generally find fund raisers more agreeable than glitzy craft shows or gallery exhibitions.

### Free Advertising

Few artists can afford to advertise. Aside from business cards and word-of-mouth they only occasionally get the opportunity to promote their work and reputation in printed media or on television. But these opportunities do arise.

I remember being in the local newspaper once every year for almost a decade with photos of myself and my carvings accompanied by an article describing my work. All it took was a call to the local paper each time there was a new reporter on staff who had not seen my work. Perhaps I was contributing a piece to a local fundraiser and the reporter felt that was newsworthy.

The first time I sold a carving over the internet I phoned the newspaper people who sent out a reporter to do a write-up. Another time I was commissioned to do a carving for a visiting dignitary. This too warranted a photo and article in the paper. When I began promoting my carving via the Internet, the subject of on-line promotion was reason enough for another article. All it takes is for the carver to exploit, sometimes even manufacture, opportunities for free advertising. Newspapers, especially the local ones, are always looking for fresh news. Why should it not be you that they write about.

## Seminars/Workshops

It is almost certainly necessary for you to teach your craft to others if you wish to promote yourself and your work. The mere fact that others value your talents enough to invite you to teach at a workshop or seminar is a real compliment, but it also puts you in contact with people who know other people who themselves have resources to open doors of opportunity for you.

Besides the excellent exposure these workshops offer, they also pay well. Most offer an hourly wage, accommodation and travel allowance. Some allow you to sell carving blanks, tools, patterns and books to supplement your income. For the most part, workshops are a busy time spiced with wonderful social interaction.

Be prepared to hunt down opportunities for teaching workshops. You will need to be able to show your credentials in word and photos, so be sure to have a "curriculum vitae" and spare prints or slides to send off in the mail. If you have an Internet connection and are able to set up a web page, you can use your web page as an on-line color brochure that is cheap to produce and available anywhere there is a phone line and a computer. Of all the promotion I have done in the last decade, nothing has come close to affording me both exposure and opportunity like the Internet.

## Starting a Carving Club

Most large cities will have a carving club that you can join. But if there isn't one close enough, start a club of your own. By using the Internet as a research tool and accessing the on-line carving community you will find there, you will be able to learn from the experiences of others the best way to start a carving club.

Carving clubs offer fellowship, support and the combined experience of others who love carving. With the combined human and financial resources of a club you can start annual carving shows-and-sales, fundraisers, workshops and competitions. With workshops and competitions, especially, you can encourage carvers to excel and mature in their craft. Of course, clubs also offer the opportunity for people to promote their work and reputation. The success of one carver benefits everyone in the club.

# BECOMING A PROFESSIONAL FULL-TIME WOODCARVER

I cannot count the number of people over the years who have asked me how they might get started carving commissions. I get regular inquiries via the Internet from people who want to strike out on their own to make a living from carving. There are also those who approach me at exhibitions and fairs who long to live the life of the independent artist.

There are many different reasons for people to pursue a career in commission woodcarving, not the least being the desire to express oneself creatively. Some wish to leave high pressure jobs in favor of self-employment in the world of crafts, where one has more control over one's life. Others desire to be their own boss. Others need to work at home where they can participate in the lives of their family.

Whatever your reason for wanting to undertake commission woodcarving, there is a way to do it properly and a way that leads to failure. I hope the insights I have gathered over 15 years of commission carving will be useful to you.

## My story

I started commission carving while I was employed as a rural parish pastor in Northern Alberta, Canada, in the late 70s. While in the parish, I used woodcarving as a means to relieve stress. I came to the conclusion after many years that the reason relief carving has this name is that it provides a person with relief from things like stress, boredom, repressed creativity, idle pastimes and the like.

It was not long after I started that a parishioner asked to buy one of my carvings. Sometime later I was asked to carve a specific theme in wood. The idea came to me that I could earn extra income through my carving, and turn this wonderful recreation into a "paying" hobby. It was the desire to expand my hobby that started me on my way as a commission woodcarver.

I carved in the basement of the parish parsonage, a space not larger that 8 feet by 12 feet, with a low ceiling and a dripping drain pipe in the corner. Soon I had earned enough money to buy more carving tools. Gradually I acquired a power saw, a router, a hand plane and a few carving instructional books. My beginnings with this craft were humble and undoubtedly less romantic than they appear after the passage of time, but I knew no different then. I was totally absorbed with my carving, and counted the hours each week until my day off when I could hide in my small shop and carve.

I did not decide to undertake commission carving as a

vocation until the day when, in order to avoid burnout, I elected to leave parish ministry. Tendering my resignation, my wife and I moved to the city with our one-year-old son, and decided that since my immediate job options were pumping gas or woodcarving, I would become a commission woodcarver.

I set up shop in the basement, behind the furnace, a step or two away from the washer and dryer. It was a tight fit. But for two years I carved in 96 square feet of "shop," sharing my elbow space with piles of wood, an old workbench I bought at auction, and a row of cupboards filled with whatever could not be store elsewhere in the house.

I had the pleasure of building a backyard shop in the third year of my artistic sojourn, and gladly left the basement behind. I now had storage racks for my wood, some proper workbenches, and two windows strategically placed to cast the right light for working in relief. I started teaching carving classes, which to my amazement not only paid well, but taught me more than I taught the students and brought in more commissions besides. In the third year AP (after parish) I began to understand that I might have something that could eventually become a vocation, maybe even a paying job. I was an entrepreneur.

My wife's ballet school was also growing by leaps and bounds by this time. So in the fifth year on our own we were able to move to a larger house where I built a larger shop, taught larger classes and carved larger carvings. I should be completely honest with you at this point. If my family were to depend completely on my carving income, we would be quite poor. I earn a good second income that nicely supplements my wife's larger income. By having a dual family income, we are financially comfortable.

Now in my sixteenth year of commission carving, and my sixteenth year of commission carving I look back and reflect on what I have learned.

## A commission woodcarver needs the following

1. A deep love for woodcarving. A person can only excel at something he enjoys. A passing interest in carving is not sufficient to make a career of it.

2. The desire to be self employed. If you want to write your own paycheck, you are on the right path. But if you can't stand the idea of not having a regular paycheck, stay away from self-employment.

3. Self discipline. If you cannot get yourself to work in the morning, nobody else will do it for you. And if you work either too hard or not hard enough, you'll either burn out or starve. Self discipline, which manifests itself in balance and moderation is a key element of success. Remember too, that professional carving is a solitary business. Self-discipline involves working comfortably on your own. Those that need social interaction to work productively will have a hard time with full-time professional commission carving.

4. The willingness to pay one's dues as an aspiring artist/craftsperson. A reputation as a reliable and capable craftsperson is earned, not bought or found by chance. It takes time for people to discover you, and even longer before you gain a reputation for being dependable, creative, trustworthy and competent. Give yourself a number of years to achieve recognition.

5. A belief that one's work has worth, and will be valued by others. My wife is the one who helps me see my carvings as my customers will eventually see them. My carving students also help me evaluate my work from the customer point of view, but I must carry the belief that my carvings are worth doing in the first place. I must value woodcarving as an art form and wood as a medium and believe that as I love woodcarvings so others will love them too.

6. The ability to learn from one's mistakes and build on one's strengths. Every mistake falls on the shoulders of the carver who made it. Some mistakes fall into the category of disasters, while others fall into the category of serendipity. With experience disasters can be avoided or at least mitigated to minor inconveniences. A carver who cannot learn from his mistakes is a carver who lives in fear of making mistakes, and for this reason is also afraid to experiment or take chances.

7. The ability to measure success/failure. Success is a difficult thing to measure unless you know what is important to you personally. If becoming rich and famous is your measure of success, you might be disappointed with this line of work. However, if you can be content with a modest income, the time spent seeing your children grow up and the satisfaction of working at what you enjoy, then this is the line of work for you.

I have concluded after many years of self-doubt that I made the right decision when I began my career as a carver. I earn a half or a third of the income of many of my friends, but I enjoy advantages that their money cannot buy. I am at home for lunch with my wife and boys every day. I can take extended summer holidays with the family. My kids know what I do for a living, and have time to know me as a person. I set my own schedule, pursue my own interests and enjoy the company of fellow carvers in my carving classes. My job is at least as secure as the jobs my friends have. My work allows my wife to pursue her work. Between the two of us we do all right financially and enjoy a close, happy family life. Big bucks could not buy what I enjoy now. With this in mind, I can rightly consider myself to be successful!

## As a novice commission woodcarver you need to:

1. Commit to the task of becoming a commission carver. Go forward. Don't look back.

2. Set a date, perhaps two years in the future, at which time you will evaluate your progress in achieving

your goals.

3. Set a goal to be achieved by the date mentioned above. Make it attainable. When I started, my goal was to be recognized in my community as a local woodcarving artist after two years had passed. When two years has passed, I sat down with my wife and some close friends to discuss if I had achieved my goal.

4. Have the basic experience you need in the various aspects of carving before you make it your career. This experience can be gathered over years of hobby carving and taking courses from more experienced carvers.

5. Have a space to carve in, the tools and equipment you need to prepare and carve wood, and the space to store supplies and materials. Also have local municipal permissions in place for doing this work out of your home, if that is where you intend to make your start. Many towns and cities require a home occupation license.

6. Set aside the time each day to carve without distraction.

7. Know how you will begin to market your carvings. If you have customers waiting for your finished carvings, all the better. Galleries, craft fairs, exhibitions, conventions, and art/craft retailers are all examples of marketing outlets.

8. Know how to do business with customers. If you cannot bring yourself to meet deadlines, deal with problems, or ask for payment, then do yourself a favor by finding some other line of work.

9. Have the cooperation and support of your spouse. My wife supports my work as I support hers. It makes good sense to work together.

10. Have a source for quality hardwood that is reliable and affordable. My preference is local white birch. It is an excellent carving wood, beautiful in so many ways and very affordable. But then I'm from Alberta, Canada, where birch is easily available.

**An advanced commission woodcarver needs to:**

1. Have a dedicated carving studio. Do not use it for fixing your car or storing your kids' bikes or doing ceramics or welding.

2. Have advanced tools and equipment for woodworking and woodcarving. A jointer, a planer, a band-saw, a table/radial arm saw, a router, a stationary sander are all examples of necessary equipment.

3. Be able to produce your own designs using your own collection of advanced drawing/design tools and equipment like light tables, pantograph, photocopier. Do not rely on others to produce your carving patterns. You must develop the skill needed to draw and design. Good patterns are not readily available commercially.

4. Have an album of photos of completed commission carvings to show customers what you have done and what can be done in woodcarving.

5. Have an inventory of patterns for stock carvings.

6. Have a collection of completed "inventory carvings" ready for display or exhibition when the opportunity presents itself.

7. Be able to acquire free publicity in your community, through the newspapers, newsletters, fairs and galleries. Every new newspaper reporter who comes to town should be seen as an opportunity for an article about an up-and-coming woodcarving artist.

8. Have business cards ready to hand out at a moment's notice.

9. Have a computer or access to one, if possible, with software to assist in the design of your carvings. A computer also allows you to prepare invoices on letterhead, to correspond by e-mail via the Internet and to create web pages.

# THE COMMISSION PROCESS

Now we get to the fun part. What do you do when you have a living, breathing, potential customer standing in front of you, asking if you could please do a carving for him? Let's take a look at the commission process from start to finish and see what it entails.

## The initial contact

The initial contact will often be over the telephone. Arrange a time for the customer to visit the studio where you can discuss the carving commission in more detail. This will allow the customer to see what you do and where you do it. It inspires confidence on the part of the customer. It gives you the opportunity to place your best foot forward.

If the commission cannot be arranged in person, then talk with the customer on the phone. When you are ready to submit preliminary designs for approval, fax the customer a copy. Everyone has access to a fax machine, if only at a local commercial fax service. What you have discussed over the phone should appear in writing on the fax document right beside the drawings that you have prepared. What is written is far less likely to be misunderstood at a later date.

## The first meeting in your studio

When the customer arrives in person at your studio, above all be business-like in a comfortable, crafty sort of way. Firm handshakes, warm greeting, eye contact and garlic-free breath all go a long way to a positive initial impression. The customer wants to meet someone who is confident in his abilities and reliable in his dealings. The customer also wants to see a "real studio," that is, one that is properly equipped, clean and organized, with real wood and real tools. The customer is curious about the carving process. You can satisfy his curiosity with what I call the "royal tour" of your studio.

When the tour is done, then it's time to get down to

business. Ask questions. Take notes. Make sketches. Clarify, clarify, clarify! Offer suggestions and alternatives that might improve the finished carving and make it more suitable to the customer's purpose.

## Commission details

1. Take notes and make drawings as reminders of the conversation you are having with the customer. I use a "Commission Sheet" that I created on the computer. It contains spaces for all the information and sketches that need to be collected for a particular carving commission. When a customer watches me fill out this sheet, he cannot help but think that I am well organized and concerned with the details.

2. Decide on the theme, purpose and style of the carving. Often a particular theme can be rendered in a number of ways. Discuss these with your customer. Inquire as to the occasion for the carving, who will receive it, where it will finally be hung, what light will it receive and be how will it be viewed.

3. Choose the wood, the size, and the shape for the carving. I always try to steer the customer toward wood that is best for the design. For example, red oak is not good for a finely detailed relief, where the coarse grain will overwhelm the detail. White birch is better, with its close grain, and its ability to hold detail and to show well in low-light situations. Red oak is better in large reliefs with bold design and absence of fine detail. There the coarse grain adds to the strength of the design.

4. Decide the budget ceiling for the commission. I charge by the square foot of finished carved area, based of the largest dimensions of the carving. That way I can quickly arrive at a cost for the customer, and the customer can understand that the cost is directly related to the work involved. To this I add the cost of the wood, measured by board feet used, and the local taxes.

Setting the budget is a delicate matter, best handled with forthrightness, fairness and scrupulous honesty. Charging by the square foot of finished carving forces you to become efficient in your carving. At this point, be sure to outline the costs that will be added to the carving commission, such as crating, taxes, installation and freight.

5. Arrange for payment in full upon delivery of the finished carving to a satisfied customer. Take no pre-payment or money down. Learn to determine which customers are trustworthy, and which are not. A simple handshake is all you need with honest people, and a contract will not be enough to force a dishonest person to pay up.

If you insist on payment only after delivery, your customers will know intuitively that you are taking a risk on their behalf. You do this to gain the confidence of your customers, and to assure them that you are interested primarily in their satisfaction. Customers will sense that only a confident and reliable artist would take this chance.

6. Set a date for the delivery, viewing and confirmation of the preliminary drawings. These drawings should be to scale, and include enough information to convey the shape, size, style and content of the finished carving. Information regarding the dimension, price, wood, delivery costs, taxes and materials should also be included with the preliminary drawings.

A preliminary design helps you and the customer arrive at a clear understanding of the commission that is about to be undertaken. It allows for revisions, corrections and minor adjustments to take place before you start working with the wood.

Keep in mind that the whole purpose of commission carving is to provide the customer with a carving suited to his particular needs while you earn an income and exercise your creative energies in the process. I like to explain to my customers that I intend to carve their idea my way. That way the customer is happy and I am happy. Carvers that expect simple acceptance of what they produce without consideration for the needs their the customer, should avoid commission carving like a plague.

7. Complete the carving. Prepare it for delivery with appropriate hangers, mounting brackets, shipping boxes and the like. Take some color print/slide photos of the carving for your records. I usually take 4-6 photos in various lighting situations and lay a small ruler or pencil beside the carving to indicate scale.

8. Arrange for the delivery of the carving. The best place to make the delivery is usually at your studio, where you can control the situation so that nothing interferes with your ability to "sell" the carving to your customer. Point out its best features, describe how the carving could best be displayed, discuss how it should be hung/mounted, and outline what the customer should do to maintain the carving. When this is done, give him the invoice and receive payment from your customer. Make sure the customer leaves with a few of your business cards to give to friends. Carry the carving to the customer's car to make sure it is not dropped, bumped or damaged with rings, zippers, buttons or car doors.

## Final considerations

If you want your reputation to spread, then remember the following:

1. Serve the customer while striving for excellence.

2. Carve what the customer wants, the way you want.

3. Believe in yourself in the same way the customer believed in you when he first asked you to do a commission carving.

4. Deliver the carving on time and on budget.

5. Maintain a clean, tidy, well organized studio and good personal hygiene.

6. Be fair to yourself and to the customer.

7. Enjoy your work and your customers.

# Woodcarvings by W.F.Judt
## Carving Commission

| Customer Name: | Date of Commission: | |
| --- | --- | --- |
| Address: | Delivery Date: | |
| Phone: | Destination of Carving: | |
| Wood Type: | Price/sq/ft | Carving Price |
| Dimensions/Shape/Area: | Crating | Taxes |
| | Delivery Cost: | Total: |
| Occasion for Carving: | | |
| Design Particulars:  _____  _____  _____  _____ | Sketches: | |

Commission sheet

# AFTERWORD

## WHY DO YOU CARVE?

This may sound like a simple question, but it is not. If you were asked by someone to explain why you carve, what would you say, and how would you phrase it? There must be some reason you carve or you would not be carving at all, right?

I hold the conviction that we do not understand something until we are able either to explain it clearly in writing or verbalize it to another person. Until then, what we think we understand is likely just a collection of feelings and thoughts loosely connected by a pattern of behaviors that may be as trite as a habit or as ardent as a conviction. Whether the reasons are shallow or deep we will not know until we attempt to put our reasons into words.

The process of articulating what is unconscious and silent is a process of self discovery. We might be quite surprised when we take the time to look at our actions and examine our behaviors to discover that we have moved beyond the point where woodcarving is a take-it-or-leave-it proposition, to the point where it has become an essential to our lifestyle, self-image and personal well-being.

Having taught carving classes for some 15 years, and having myself carved for over 22 years, I have had opportunity to observe and identify a variety of reasons why people carve. From what I can see, the reasons fall into four general categories as follows:

1. People carve to relieve stress.
2. People carve in response to a need to be creative.
3. People carve for the companionship of other carvers.
4. People carve to satisfy a competitive urge.

Let me illustrate point number one: One of my carving students is a psychiatrist at the local hospital. He is a native of South Africa, now five years in this country of long dark winters and short bright summers. He is a self-confessed obsessive-compulsive who carves primarily to relieve the stress of his very demanding profession. He is a very slow carver. In the past, I would pester him to carve more quickly so that he could complete a project within the ten weeks of a single course, thinking for sure that he would appreciate my concern for his finances. One day he quietly told me that he enjoyed carving slowly. It was therapeutic.

From that time on I have allowed him to carve at his own speed, but now I pester him about how I should be charging him "therapy rates" or at least extra-billing Health Care for the services being rendered to him in carving class. In this regard he merely laughs and wishes me luck.

Now let me illustrate point number two: I have another carving student whose job it is to maintain the Catholic School buildings in our region. This man works with his hands and manages contractors, juggles projects and supervises day-to-day maintenance with a never ending list of things to make, repair, install and maintain. He likes his work, but it consists mainly of "putting out fires."

He carves in order to explore his creative side. I know each time he approaches me with a new carving idea for which we will then work up a design that it will be a challenge from start to finish. When he carves, he carves from the heart, with great intensity, sweat on his brow, his mind moving between apprehension and joy as the carving passes through various stages. This man needs to be creative. He needs to express in wood what he feels inside his soul. It is for himself that he carves, not for anyone else. It is his agenda that he follows. And when his carving is done he smiles a smile that is as wide as all outdoors.

Now let me illustrate point number three: One of my "lifers," a man who has enrolled in every carving class I have offered in the last 14 years, is a talented carver and a wonderful technician. His carvings are clean and smooth. He likes carvings that have that "warm and fuzzy" feeling, like the one of a father holding his little baby in his hands or a couple of intertwining hearts decorated with flowers and butterflies and ribbons. Most of his carvings he gives away to delighted relatives who make sure he knows how much they would like one of his pieces.

This fellow comes to class primarily because he enjoys the company of fellow carvers. The social aspects of a carving class, where he is in the company of friends, some of whom he has known for over a decade, are very important to him.

In carving class he can immerse himself in his project, take time to share the latest jokes from the workplace, visit with his friends, and from time to time, share his burdens with people who understand where he is coming from.

Finally, point number four: There are carvers who carve to compete. Pure and simple. They want to be the best, and they relish the challenge of competition. No investment of time is too much, and no tool is spared in order to surpass the efforts of their peers. This type of carver generally plays his cards pretty close to his chest, not sharing secrets that could give the other competitors an edge. Among his friends are carvers who also compete, and between them is a genuine camaraderie.

Now, back to the question: Why do YOU carve? Stress-management? Creative impulse? Companionship? Competitive drive?

When I first began to carve, it did not matter what I carved, as long as the chips were flying. Years passed and I found that I was carving to creatively express my Christian faith, on one side, and to relieve the stress of work on the other. I had begun to gather tools, equipment and skills together so that I was making more than just a pile of chips.

One day I found that I was carving in order to make a living. I had left my former job and needed time to get past what amounted to a condition of burnout. So while I was carving to earn a living, I was also carving to heal myself. But carving served a new function. It now had to pay its way.

Healing came, and when I was convinced that I could make a go of it as a woodcarver, I made the decision to stay with it. At this point I entered into a creative stage, where I was carving not only to earn a living, but to express myself in the medium of wood. I carved what was important to me. Even when I carved commission projects for others, I still carved their ideas my way. I was still able to be creative within the confines of the commission process.

Now I carve because I have discovered, after two decades of working in relief, that I have acquired a collection of skills and a repertoire of designs that allow me to do pretty well whatever I want in relief. I see no barriers that are insurmountable. I see no limits to what can, with time and perseverance, be rendered in relief. It feels like I now have wings to fly, whereas in the past I felt like a fledgling flapping its wings but not taking to flight. Now I feel like an adult in my craft, fully fledged and able to mount the currents of creativity to heights never before attained. It's the thrill of achieving new heights that now motivates me.

But I also carve because I believe it is a calling. That may sound silly to you, but that's the way I see it. Some are called to teach, others to heal, others to lead, still others to nourish. I was called to carve, and in so doing to bring joy, pleasure and meaning into the lives of those who own my carvings and who participate in my carving classes.

I don't make carvings, really. I fashion family heirlooms that will be handed down through the generations. I create testaments to faith and conviction. I create gifts that, for the giver, communicate love, devotion and affection. Sometimes all that my carvings communicate is the gratitude of the giver. Sometimes, though, they contain a lifetime of memories modeled in wood for generations to ponder.

Carving is no longer something I merely do. It is something I am obligated, compelled, thrilled, and inspired to do. It is something for which I am grateful and yet for which I feel entrusted. I can relate well to the biblical story of the servant who was entrusted with his master's possessions and whose stewardship would be held up to account when his master returned.

So, why do YOU carve?

Answer this question and you will open doors to self understanding that are otherwise closed. One ancient philosopher say... "Know thyself." And another said "To thine own self be true." I'm not a philosopher. But I do know that we have to be able to put it into words why we carve if our carving is going to take on new dimensions of meaning and purpose.

## AERO
ABCDEFGHIJKLMNOPQRSTUVWXYZ
abcdefghijklmnopqrstuvwxyz
0123456789

## BOOKMAN OLD STYLE BOLD
ABCDEFGHIJKLMNOPQRSTUVWXYZ
abcdefghijklmnopqrstuvwxyz
0123456789

## BUCKINGHAM BOLD
ABCDEFGHIJKLMNOPQRSTUVWXYZ
abcdefghijklmnopqrstuvwxyz
0123456789

## CALLIGRAPHIC
ABCDEFGHIJKLMNOPQRSTUVWXYZ
abcdefghijklmnopqrstuvwxyz
0123456789

## CAXTON BOLD
ABCDEFGHIJKLMNOPQRSTUVWXYZ
abcdefghijklmnopqrstuvwxyz
0123456789

## CHARCOAL
ABCDEFGHIJKLMNOPQRSTUVWXYZ
abcdefghijklmnopqrstuvwxyz
0123456789

## HELVETICA BLACK

**ABCDEFGHIJKLMNOPQRSTUVWXYZ**

**abcdefghijklmnopqrstuvwxyz**

**0123456789**

## LIFFO

ABCDEFGHIJKLMNOPQRSTUVWXYZ

0123456789

## TEXTILE

*ABCDEFGHIJKLMNOPQRSTUVWXYZ*

*abcdefghijklmnopqrstuvwxyz*

*0123456789*

## URWTYPEWRITER

**ABCDEFGHIJKLMNOPQRSTUVWXYZ**

**abcdefghijklmnopqrstuvwxyz**

**0123456789**

## ZAPF CHANCERY

*ABCDEFGHIJKLMNOPQRSTUVWXYZ*

*abcdefghijklmnopqrstuvwxyz*

*0123456789*

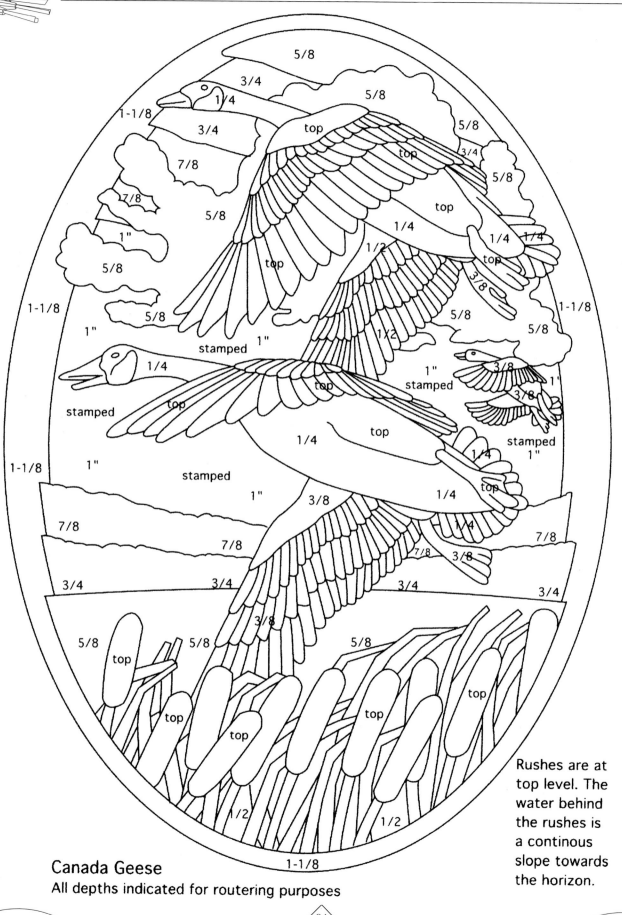

5/8

3/4

5/8

1/4

5/8

top

1-1/8

top

3/4

5/8

3/4

7/8

top

5/8

7/8

top

1/4

5/8

1/4    1/4

1"

1/2

top

5/8

top

3/8

5/8

1-1/8

1"

5/8

5/8

stamped

1"

1/2

1-1/8

1/4

top

top

1"

3/8

stamped

1/4

1"

stamped

top

1/4

1"

top

stamped

1"

7/8

1/4

1-1/8

1"

stamped

1"

3/8

1/4

7/8

7/8

7/8

3/8

7/8

3/4

3/4

3/4

3/4

3/8

5/8

top

5/8

5/8

5/8

top

top

top

top

top

1/2

1/2

1-1/8

**Canada Geese**
All depths indicated for routering purposes

Rushes are at
top level. The
water behind
the rushes is
a continous
slope towards
the horizon.

Stamped
Background

Dashed lines
indicate router
depths

**Dophins**
All depths indicated are for routering purposes

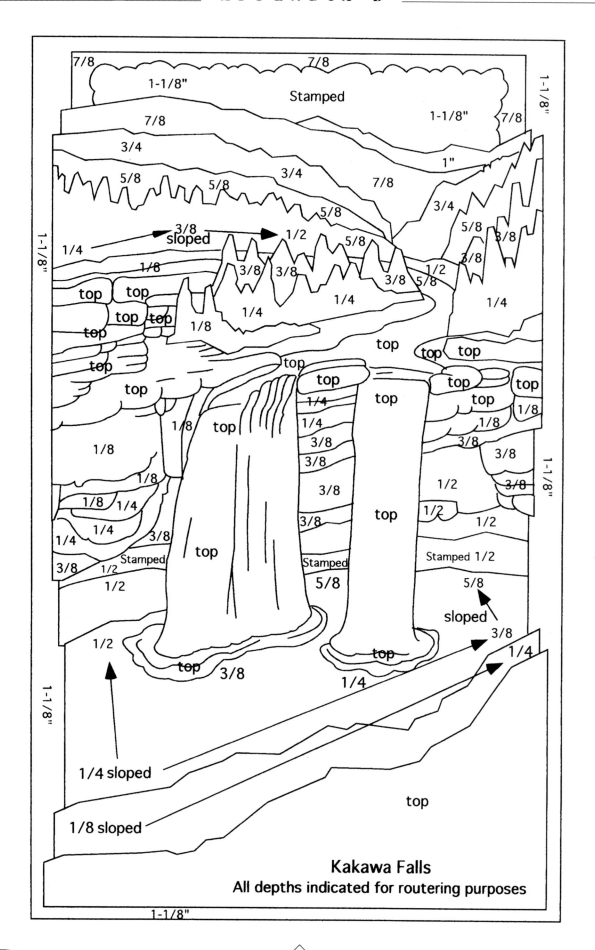

Kakawa Falls
All depths indicated for routering purposes

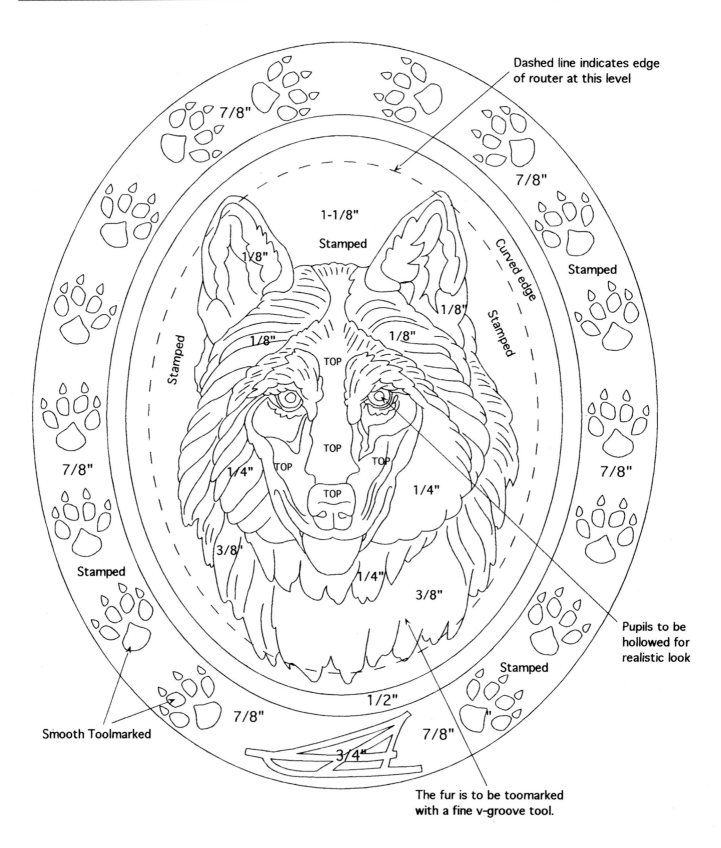

Dashed line indicates edge of router at this level

7/8"

7/8"

1-1/8"

Stamped

Stamped

1/8"

Curved edge

1/8"

Stamped

Stamped

1/8"

1/8"

Stamped

1/8"

TOP

TOP

TOP

TOP

7/8"

7/8"

1/4"

TOP

TOP

1/4"

Pupils to be hollowed for realistic look

3/8"

Stamped

1/4"

3/8"

7/8"

Stamped

Smooth Toolmarked

1/2"

7/8"

7/8"

3/4"

The fur is to be toomarked with a fine v-groove tool.

## Malamute: Sled Dog
All depths indicated are for routering purposes

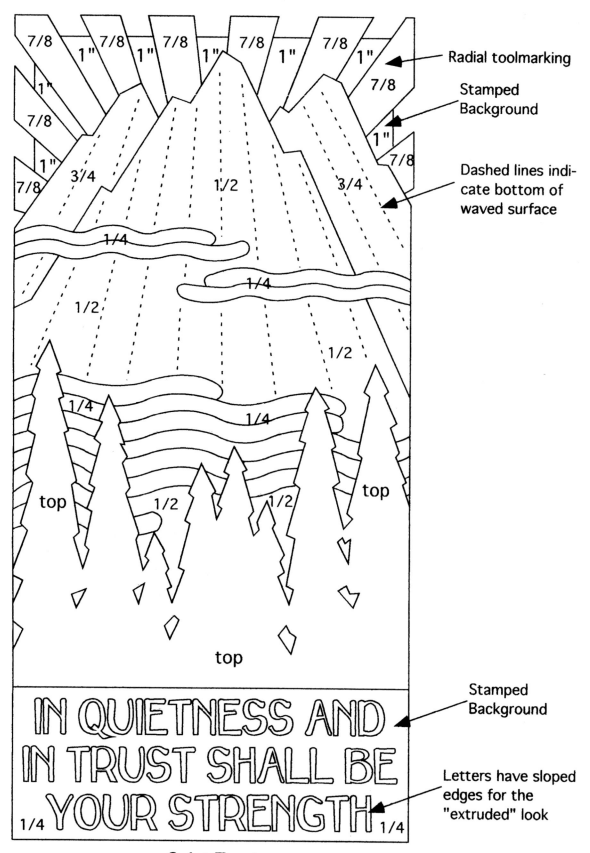

Radial toolmarking

Stamped Background

Dashed lines indicate bottom of waved surface

Stamped Background

Letters have sloped edges for the "extruded" look

**Quiet Trust**
**All depths indicated are for routering purposes**

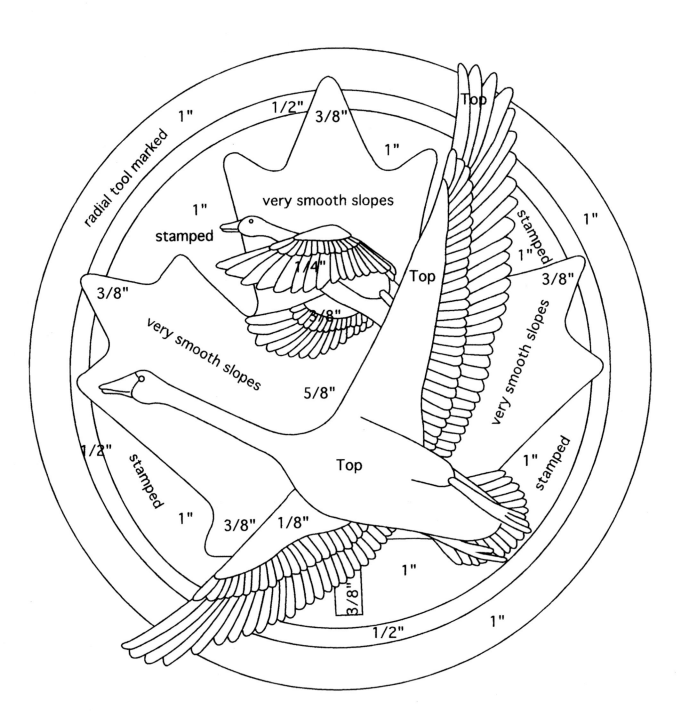

**Trumpeter Swan and Mallard**
All depths indicated are for routering purposes

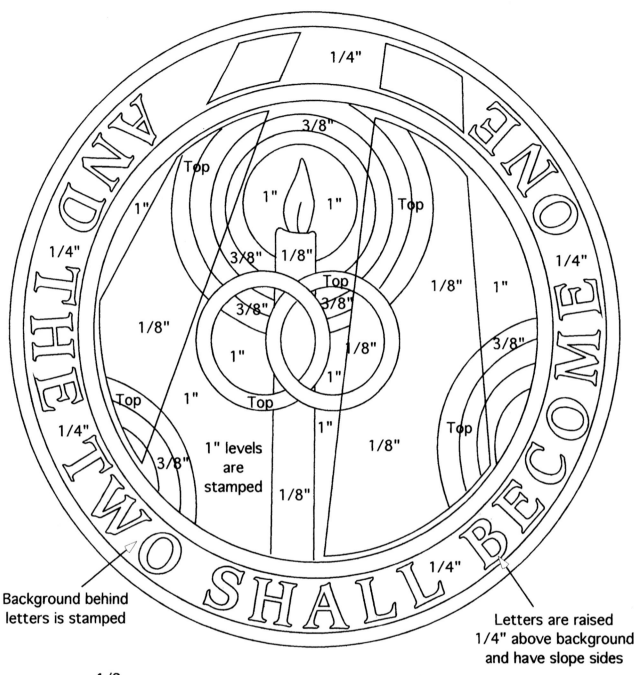

1/4"

3/8"

Top

1"     1"

Top

1/4"

1/8"

3/8"   1/8"

Top

1/8"   1"

3/8"

3/8"   3/8"

Top

1/8"

1"     1"

1"     1"

Top

1/4"

1/8"

1/4"

3/8"

1" levels
are
stamped

Top

1/8"

1"

1/8"

1/4"

Background behind
letters is stamped

Letters are raised
1/4" above background
and have slope sides

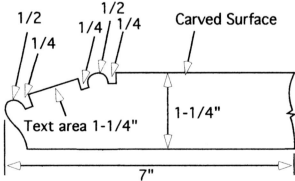

1/2

1/4

1/2

1/4  1/4

Carved Surface

1-1/4"

Text area 1-1/4"

7"

Half-Cross-section of Turned Plate

**Wedding Plate**
Turned Plate
14" daimeter

All depths indicated are for routering purposes

# Tool profiles for Straight Chisels, Gouges and V-tools

### Skew
- 2mm
- 3mm
- 5mm
- 8mm
- 12mm
- 16mm
- 20mm
- 25mm
- 30mm

### 1
- 2mm
- 3mm
- 5mm
- 8mm
- 12mm
- 16mm
- 20mm
- 25mm
- 30mm

### 2
- 2mm
- 3mm
- 5mm
- 8mm
- 12mm
- 16mm
- 20mm
- 25mm
- 30mm

### 3
- 3mm
- 5mm
- 8mm
- 12mm
- 16mm
- 20mm
- 25mm
- 30mm

### 5
- 2mm
- 3mm
- 5mm
- 12mm
- 16mm
- 20mm
- 25mm
- 30mm

### 7
- 3mm
- 5mm
- 10mm
- 12mm
- 16mm
- 20mm
- 25mm
- 30mm

### 9
- 2mm
- 3mm
- 5mm
- 7mm
- 10mm
- 12mm
- 16mm
- 20mm
- 25mm
- 30mm

### 11
- 2mm
- 3mm
- 4mm
- 5mm
- 7mm
- 10mm
- 15mm
- 18mm
- 25mm
- 30mm

### V-tool
- 2mm
- 3mm
- 4mm
- 6mm
- 8mm
- 10mm
- 20mm

# ABOUT THE AUTHOR

W.F. (Bill) Judt has been carving nearly a quarter century, starting with an adult night school course offered by the Winnipeg School Board in 1975. Mostly self-taught, he has carved in the relative isolation of northern Alberta, and his style of carving is quite different from that of carvers elsewhere.

He specializes in relief carving in panels that are 2" thick or less. Almost all of his carvings are done on a commission basis and are purchased by private families, businesses and corporations. Bill has recently begun teaching workshops through the Alberta Rocky Mountain Carving Seminar, an annual event hosted by Red Deer College's Summer Series program. He also teaches evening classes throughout the school year out of his home-based studio.

He is heavily involved in promoting woodcarving on the Internet. He owns and operates the Woodcarver Mailing List and also publishes the bi-monthly on-line magazine "WWWoodc@rver E-zine." His was the first woodcarving web site on the internet located at:

*http://www.WWWoodcarver.com/*

In 1997 he authored his first book *Relief Carving Treasury,* published by Fox Chapel Publishing Company. He has written many articles for various carving publications, including *Wood Carving Illustrated* and *Chip Chats* magazines.

Bill lives with his family in Saskatoon, Saskatchewan, Canada, where he maintains his carving studio. He and his wife have two sons.

# Books by the Experts

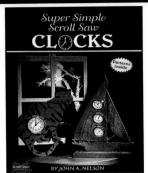
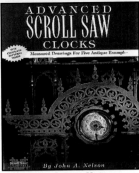

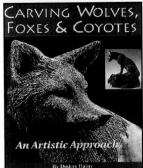

# More Books by the Experts

**Carving the Human Face**
*By Jeff Phares*
The best book available on carving faces! A full color guide is included.
*104 pages, 8.5x11", soft cover.*
**$24.95** • 1-56523-102-3

**Fireplace & Mantel Ideas**
*By John Lewman*
15 ready-to-use patterns and hundreds of photos showing installation and design.
*90 pages, 8.5x11, soft cover.*
**$19.95** • 1-56523-106-6

**Scroll Saw Relief Projects**
*By Marilyn Carmin*
The first book on fret and relief work. Includes more than 100 patterns.
*120 pages, 8.5x11, soft cover.*
**$14.95** • 1-56523-107-4

**Carving Crazy Kritters**
*By Gary Batte*
Full of creative new designs for caricature animals. A real winner!
*64 pages, 8.5x11, soft cover.*
**$14.95** • 1-56523-114-7

**Creative Christmas Carvings**
*By Tina Toney*
A beautiful and practical full-color guide to exciting holiday carving projects.
*64 pages, 8.5x11, soft cover.*
**$14.95** • 1-56523-120-1

**Scroll Saw Fretwork Patterns ~ Dog Breeds**
*By Judy Gale Roberts*
Includes dozens of all-new designs of "man's best friend".
*60 pages, 8.5x11, soft cover-spiral bound.*
**$16.95** • 1-883083-08-7

**Scroll Saw Christmas Ornaments**
*By Tom Zieg*
Over 200 ornament patterns, with brass, copper and plastic designs.
*64 pages, 8.5x11, soft cover.*
**$9.95** • 1-56523-123-6

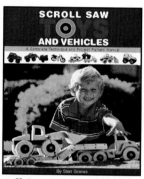

**Scroll Saw Toys and Vehicles Technique & Pattern Manual**
*By Stan Graves*
Create easy, fun toys on your scroll saw with everyday materials.
*56 pages, 8.5x11, soft cover.*
**$12.95** • 1-56523-115-5

**Relief Carving ~ Patterns, Tips & Techniques**
*By William F. Judt*
A complete introduction to relief carving. Learn tricks of the trade!
*120 pages, 8.5x11, soft cover.*
**$19.95** • 1-56523-124-4

**Scroll Saw Art Puzzles**
*By Tony and June Burns*
Includes 32 patterns for cute, classical and whimsical puzzles.
*80 pages, 8.5x11, soft cover.*
**$14.95** • 1-56523-116-3

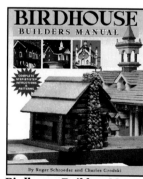

**Birdhouse Builders Manual**
*By Roger Schroeder and Charles Grodshi*
Full patterns, step-by-step photos and instructions. Sure to please!
*120 pages, 8.5x11, soft cover.*
**$19.95** • 1-56523-100-7

**Scroll Saw Workbook**
*By John Nelson*
The best beginner's technique book from noted author John Nelson.
*96 pages, 8.5x11, soft cover.*
**$14.95** • 1-56523-117-1

**Western Scroll Saw and Inlay Patterns**
*By Joe Paisley*
Exciting new inlay techniques and lots of new western patterns.
*100 pages, 8.5x11, soft cover.*
**$14.95** • 1-56523-118-X

Stunning coffee table book!

**Wood Sculptures ~ Expressions In Wood**
*By J. Christopher White*
Stylized carved wooden sculpture at its best.
*128 pages, 9x12, hard cover.*
**$34.95** • 1-56523-122-8

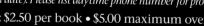

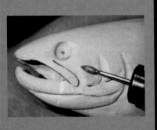